THE CONSTANT COUPLE

by George Farquhar

(A TRIP TO THE JUBILEE)

A programme/text with commentary by Simon Trussler

Contents

Royal Shakespeare Company ii
The Cast iii
The Actors iv, v, vi
RSC Theatres vii
Staff and Acknowledgements viii
Stage History ix
George Farquhar: a Brief Chronology and
A Context for *The Constant Couple* x, xi
Farquhar and the War of the Theatres xii
The Wits, the Cits, and Jeremy Collier xiii
The City End and the Court End xiv
Cash and Class – or 'Pounds per Annum' xv
Writers and Critics on Farquhar xvi
The Pocket-Book of Alderman Smuggler xvii
For Further Reading xviii
Interior of the Swan Theatre xix
Director's Note by Roger Michell xx
The Constant Couple xxi

Swan Theatre Plays published by Methuen London
by arrangement with the Royal Shakespeare Company

The Royal Shakespeare Company (RSC), is the title under which the Royal Shakespeare Theatre, Stratford-upon-Avon, has operated since 1961. Now one of the best-known theatre companies in the world, the RSC builds on a long and distinguished history of theatre in Stratford-upon-Avon.

In essence, the aim of the Company is the same as that expressed in 1905 by Sir Frank Benson, then director of the Stratford theatre: 'to train a company, every member of which would be an essential part of a homogeneous whole, consecrated to the practice of the dramatic arts and especially to the representation of the plays of Shakespeare'. The RSC is formed around a core of associate artists – actors, directors, designers and others – with the aim that their different skills should combine, over the years, to produce a distinctive approach to theatre, both classical and modern.

When, just a year after the granting, in 1925, of its Royal Charter, the theatre was almost completely destroyed by fire, a worldwide campaign was launched to build a new one. Productions moved to a local cinema until the new theatre, designed by Elisabeth Scott, was opened by the Prince of Wales on 23 April, 1932. Over the next thirty years, under the influence of directors such as Robert Atkins, Bridges-Adams, Iden Payne, Komisarjevsky, Sir Barry Jackson, Glen Byam Shaw and Anthony Quayle, the Shakespeare Memorial Theatre maintained a worldwide reputation.

In 1960, the newly appointed artistic director, Peter Hall, extended the re-named Royal Shakespeare Company's operations to include a London base at the Aldwych Theatre, and widened the Company's repertoire to include modern as well as classical work. Other innovations of the period which have shaped today's Company were the travelling Theatre-goround and experimental work which included the Theatre of Cruelty season.

Under Trevor Nunn, who took over as artistic director in 1968, this experimental work in small performance spaces led, in 1974, to the opening of The Other Place, Stratford-upon-Avon. This was a rehearsal space converted into a theatre and in 1977 its London counterpart, The Warehouse, opened with a policy of presenting new British plays. In the same year the RSC played its first season in Newcastle upon Tyne – now an annual event. In 1978, the year in which Terry Hands joined Trevor Nunn as artistic director, the RSC also fulfilled an ambition to tour towns and villages with little or no access to live professional theatre.

In 1982, the RSC moved its London base to the Barbican Centre in the City of London, opening both the Barbican Theatre, specially built for the RSC by the generosity of the Corporation of the City of London, and The Pit, a small theatre converted like The Warehouse and The Other Place, from a rehearsal room.

The 1986 season saw the opening of this new RSC theatre: the Swan. Built within the section of the shell of the original Shakespeare Memorial Theatre which escaped the 1926 fire, the Swan is a Jacobean-style playhouse staging the once hugely popular but now rarely-seen plays of Shakespeare's contemporaries during the period 1570-1750. This new dimension to the Royal Shakespeare Company's work has been made possible by the extremely generous gift of Frederick R. Koch, the RSC's benefactor. In 1987 the RSC, supported by Frank and Woji Gero and Playhouse Productions, and by Eddie Kulukundis, presented a season at the Mermaid Theatre, London, which included the Swan repertoire and two American plays. In early 1987 Terry Hands became sole Artistic Director and Chief Executive of the Company.

Throughout its history, the RSC has augmented its central operations with national and international tours, films, television programmes, commercial transfers and fringe activities. It has won over 200 national and international awards including most recently the Queen's Award for Export – but despite box office figures which, it is thought, have no equal anywhere in the world, the costs of RSC activities cannot be recouped from ticket sales alone. We rely on assistance from the Arts Council of Great Britain, amounting to about 40% of our costs in any one year, from work in other media and, increasingly, from commercial sponsorship. To find out more about the RSC's activities and to make sure of priority booking for our productions, why not become a member of the Company's Mailing List. Details of how to apply can be found in the theatre foyer.

CAST IN ORDER OF APPEARANCE

Footmen	**Stephen Jacobs**
	Peter Lennon
	James Purefoy
	Ken Shorter
	David Solomon
	Melanie Thaw
Vizard	**David Acton**

outwardly pious, otherwise a great debauchee, and villainous

Alderman Smuggler	**Joe Melia**

an old Merchant

Colonel Standard	**Tony Armatrading**

a disbanded Colonel, brave and generous

Sir Harry Wildair	**Pip Donaghy**

an airy gentleman, affecting humorous gaiety and freedom in his behaviour

Clincher Senior	**Simon Russell Beale**

a pert London 'prentice turned Beau, and affecting travel

Lady Lurewell	**Maureen Beattie**

a Lady of a jilting temper, proceeding from a resentment of her wrongs from Men

Parly	**Jenni George**

Maid to Lady Lurewell

Clincher Junior	**Mark Sproston**

a Brother, educated in the Country

Dicky	**Stephen Jacobs**

his Man

Lady Darling	**Jill Spurrier**

an old Lady, Mother to Angelica

Angelica	**Amanda Root**

a Woman of Honour

Tom Errand	**Desmond Barrit**

a Porter

Tom Errand's Wife	**Claudette Williams**
Constable	**Ken Shorter**
Butler	**Peter Lennon**

Directed by	**Roger Michell**
Designed by	**Ultz**
Lighting by	**Wayne Dowdeswell**
Music by	**Jeremy Sams**
Choreography by	**Pat Garrett**
Music Director	**John Woolf**
Assistant Director	**Stephen Rayne**
Assistants to the Designer	**Nicky Gillibrand, Jeremy Herbert**
Company voice work by	**Cicely Berry** and **Andrew Wade**
Stage Manager	**Rachael Whitteridge**
Deputy Stage Manager	**Sheonagh Darby**
Assistant Stage Manager	**Philip Chard**

Understudies

Desmond Barrit Smuggler
Stephen Jacobs Clincher Junior
Peter Lennon Clincher Senior
James Purefoy Standard
Ken Shorter Tom Errand
David Solomon Vizard/Dicky
Mark Sproston Wildair
Jill Spurrier Tom Errand's Wife
Melanie Thaw Lady Lurewell/Angelica
Claudette Williams Lady Darling/Parly

The performance is approximately 2½ hours in length, including one interval of fifteen minutes.

First performance of this production: Swan Theatre, Stratford-upon-Avon, 30 March 1988.

Please do not smoke or use cameras or tape recorders in the auditorium. And please remember that noise such as whispering, coughing, rustling programmes and the bleeping of digital watches can be distracting to performers and also spoils the performance for other members of the audience.

Biographies

DAVID ACTON *Vizard*

Theatre: Seasons at Newbury, Basingstoke, Southampton, York, Bolton, Durham, including Algernon in *The Importance of Being Earnest*, Angel in *Clouds*, Hibbert in *Journey's End*, Charles Lomax in *Major Barbara*, Edgar in *King Lear*, Arcite in *The Two Noble Kinsmen*, Romeo in *Romeo and Juliet*, *The Trial* (Cherub Company), Moirron in *Moliere* (Gate At The Latchmere), St George in *Down by the Greenwood Side* (Donmar Warehouse), Maugrim in *The Lion, The Witch and The Wardrobe* (Westminster), *The Oresteia* and *Serjeant Musgrave's Dance* (NT); UK tours: Title role in *Hamlet* (Oxford Playhouse Co.). Tours abroad: Billy in *The Real Thing* (Watermill Theatre Co.), *Tonight at 8.30* (Vienna English Theatre).
RSC: Angelo in *The Comedy of Errors*, Rosencrantz in *Hamlet* (RSC NatWest tour 1987). This season: Vizard in *The Constant Couple*, Shoemaker in *The Man of Mode*.

TONY ARMATRADING *Colonel Standard*

Theatre: Male Nurse in *Whose Life Is It Anyway?* (Birmingham & Coventry), *Antigone, Cinderella*, Telephone Man in *Barefoot in the Park*, *Joseph and the Amazing Technicolor Dreamcoat* (Croydon), Jelly Roll Morton in *Jelly Roll Soul* (Deptford Albany and tour), *Smile Orange, Hansel and Gretel, Moon On A Rainbow Shawl* (Stratford East), *Measure for Measure* (NT).
RSC: Sancho in *The Rover*, Joffer/Second Captain in *The Fair Maid of the West*, Scipio in *The Great White Hope*, Tybalt in *Romeo and Juliet*, Belvile in *The Rover*. This season: Standard in *The Constant Couple*, Banquo in *Macbeth*.
Television: *Angels, Grange Hill, Empire Road, Alive and Kicking, A Taste of Honey, Cats Eyes, Let's Pretend, Gems, Casualty*.
Radio: *Some Kind of Hero, The Wasted Years*.

DESMOND BARRIT *Tom Errand*

Theatre: Seasons at Chichester, Lincoln, Swansea, York, Cardiff, East Grinstead, including 1st Player in *Rosencrantz and Guildenstern Are Dead*, Pozzo in *Waiting for Godot*, Lady Bracknell in *The Importance of Being Earnest*, Dr Emmerson in *Whose Life Is It Anyway?* Sir Toby Belch in *Twelfth Night*, Common Man in *A Man For All Seasons*, Snoopy in *You're A Good Man, Charlie Brown*, George Crofts in *Mrs Warren's Profession*, Charlie in *Three Men on a Horse* (NT/Vaudeville), Achille Blond in *The Magistrate*, Chauffeur in *Jacobowsky and the Colonel* (NT), Brogard in *The Scarlet Pimpernel* (Her Majesty's), Father in *Respectable Wedding* (King's Head). UK tours: *The Boyfriend, Sunshine Boys* and *Joseph and the Amazing Technicolor Dreamcoat*.
RSC: This season: Tom Errand in *The Constant Couple*, Ross/Porter in *Macbeth*, Trinculo in *The Tempest*.
Television: *Valentine Park, Bowen and Partners, QT, Crossroads, Let Dogs Delight, Follow The Star, Roof Over Your Head*. **Film:** *Lassiter*.
Other: Pantomime Dame, and charity pantomime *The Earth Awakes*.

SIMON RUSSELL BEALE *Clincher Senior*

Theatre: Theobald Maske in *Die Hose, Points of Departure*, Sandra in *Sandra/Manon, The Death of Elias Sawney* (Traverse Theatre, Edinburgh), Osric in *Hamlet* (Lyceum, Edinburgh), *Look to the Rainbow* (London), The Ward in *Women Beware Women* (Royal Court).
RSC: Young Shepherd in *The Winter's Tale*, Ed Kno'well in *Every Man in His*

Humour, Oliver in *The Art of Success*, Fawcett in *The Fair Maid of the West*, Kuligin in *The Storm*, Nick in *Speculators*. This season: Clincher Senior in *The Constant Couple*, Sir Fopling Flutter in *The Man of Mode*, Bob Hedges in *Restoration*. **Television:** *A Very Peculiar Practice*.

MAUREEN BEATTIE *Lady Lurewell*

Theatre: Seasons at Dundee, Perth, Edinburgh, Coventry, Manchester, Glasgow, including title role in *Major Barbara*, Judith in *The Innocents*, Rosalind in *As You Like It*, Pegeen Mike in *Playboy of the Western World*, Lady Macbeth in *Macbeth*, Portia in *The Merchant of Venice*, Isabella in *Edward II*, Emilia in *Othello* (Lyric, Hammersmith), Headmistress in *Daisy Pulls It Off* (Globe). Scottish tour as Titania in *A Midsummer Night's Dream*. Tour to Lanzarote and Edinburgh Festival '87 in *Marie of Scotland* with own theatre company.
RSC: Tour abroad in *The Hollow Crown*. This season: Lady Lurewell in *The Constant Couple*, Lady Macduff in *Macbeth*, Pert in *The Man of Mode*.
Television: *Truckers, Troubles and Strife, The Campbells*.
Radio: *Can You Hear Me?* (Pye Radio Best Actress award 1981).
Other: Formed own theatre company with partner Judy Sweeney called Swaive Kinooziers.

PIP DONAGHY *Sir Harry Wildair*

Theatre: Seasons at Sheffield, Nottingham, Cambridge and Liverpool. Jesus Christ in *The Passion*, Clytemnestra in *The Oresteia*, Sir Lucius O' Trigger in *The Rivals*, Napoleon in *Animal Farm*, *The Wandering Jew, Countrymania* (NT). UK tours: *Waiting for Godot*, (with Not the National Theatre), *The Speakers, Fanshen, Devil's Island, Say Your Prayers* (with Joint Stock), *Bitter Apples, Trees in the Wind, The Garden of England* (with 7:84). Tours abroad: *The Oresteia* (Epidaurus).
RSC: This season: Sir Harry Wildair in *The Constant Couple*, Medley in *The Man of Mode*.
Television: *Invisible Man, Pickwick Papers, Oliver Twist, Alice in Wonderland*. **Film:** *1984*.

WAYNE DOWDESWELL *Lighting*

Theatre: *The Fantasticks, Salad Days*, Verdi's *Macbeth, Nabucco* and *Aida*, Mozart's *Cosi Fan Tutte, Don Giovanni* (Sheffield University Theatre), *No More Sitting on the Old School Bench, Painted Veg and Parkinson, Fanshen, The Hunchback of Notre Dame* (Manchester Contact Theatre).
RSC: Joined the RSC in 1978. Worked at TOP as Deputy Chief Electrician and Chief Electrician. TOP productions include *Money, Golden Girls, Desert Air, Today, The Dillen, Mary After the Queen, The Quest*. Currently Resident Lighting Designer at the Swan Theatre – *The Two Noble Kinsmen, Every Man In His Humour, The Rover, The Fair Maid of the West. Hyde Park, Titus Andronicus, The Jew of Malta, The New Inn*. This season: *The Constant Couple*.

PAT GARRETT *Choreography*

Trained as a dancer. Taught on performing arts degree at Leicester Polytechnic. Guest teacher for a number of dance companies. She has choreographed a large number of dance pieces for a variety of dance groups and has received commissions from the Arts Council of Great Britain.
Theatre: *Master Class* (Leicester Haymarket, London & UK tour), *The Glass Menagerie* (Studio Theatre, Leicester), *The London Cuckolds*

(Leicester Haymarket & Lyric Hammersmith), *The Ass, Needles of Light* (Foco Novo – UK tour & Riverside Studios), *The Country Wife* (Coventry), *Tom Jones* (Derby Playhouse), *A Piece of My Mind* (Southampton & London) *The Gingerbread Man, The Decameron, Love Off the Shelf* (Southampton).
Film: *Goodie-Two-Shoes, The Little Shop of Horrors, Santa Claus – The Movie.*

JENNI GEORGE *Parly*
Theatre: Seasons at Leeds, Manchester and Ipswich, including *A Midsummer Night's Dream*, Biddy in *Great Expectations*, Tweeny in *The Admirable Crichton*, *Cymbeline*, Maria in *Twelfth Night*, Adriana in *The Comedy of Errors*, Josephine Baker in *Piaf*, Alea in *Split Second* (Lyric, Hammersmith). UK Tour of *Getting Plenty* (Temba Theatre Group).
RSC: Second Queen in *The Two Noble Kinsmen*, Callis in *The Rover*, Queen Tota in *The Fair Maid of the West*, Anna in *Dido and Aeneas*, Peacemaker (RSC Festival). This season: Parly in *The Constant Couple*, Emilia in *The Man of Mode*, Niobe in *The Love of the Nightingale*.
Television: *Jury, Just Good Friends, Johnny Jarvis, Frontline, In Sickness and In Health.*

STEVEN JACOBS *Dicky/Footman*
Theatre: *Good Lads at Heart* (National Youth Theatre, New York). Seasons at Chester, Basingstoke, Ipswich and Scarborough. Trip in *The School for Scandal* (Haymarket/Duke of Yorks), Pepe in *El Senor Gallindez* (Gate Theatre), O'Connor in *Cards on the Table* (Churchill, Bromley), *Red Devil Battery Sign* (Roundhouse). *State of Affairs* (UK tour). Tour of Belgium with English Teaching Theatre, *The Provok'd Wife* (Austrian tour), *The School for Scandal* (Europe and Turkey).
RSC: This season: Dicky in *The Constant Couple*, Lennox in *Macbeth*, Adrian in *The Tempest*.
Television: *Full House, Never the Twain, Case of the Frightened Lady, Murder of a Moderate Man, Dempsey and Makepeace, Heather Ann, Jemima Shore Investigates, Mapp and Lucia.*
Film: *Break Out.*

PETER LENNON *Butler/Footman*
Theatre: Theseus in *A Midsummer Night's Dream*, Host of The Garter in *The Merry Wives of Windsor* (Open Air Theatre), *The Taming of the Shrew* (Nottingham), Paradise in *Bashville* (Open Air Theatre and Birmingham).
RSC: *Twelfth Night, Julius Caesar, The Comedy of Errors, Measure for Measure, Space Invaders, Les Liaisons Dangereuses* (West End). This season: Butler in *The Constant Couple*, Menteith in *Macbeth*.

JOE MELIA *Alderman Smuggler*
Theatre: *One to Another, Irma La Douce, Beyond The Fringe, Happy End, A Day in the Death of Joe Egg, Trixie and Baba, Who's Who of Flapland, Leonardo's Last Supper, Noonday Demons, Enter Solly Gold, Rabelais, The Sandboy, The Threepenny Opera, Who's Who, Aladdin, Birds of Passage, Number One* (London).
RSC: Ubell Untermeyer in *Section 9*, Froylan in *The Bewitched*, Bill in *The Can-Opener*, Sgt Fielding in *Too True to be Good*, John Dory in *Wild Oats*, Len Bonny in *Privates on Parade*, Touchstone in *As You Like It*, Second Murderer in *Richard III*, Thersites in *Troilus and Cressida*, *The Swan Down Gloves*, Maurice in *Good*, Isaac Levine in *Flight*, Autolycus in *The Winter's Tale*, Sir Robert Walpole in *The Art of Success*, Mayor/Mullisheg, King of Fez in *The Fair Maid of the West*, Chief of Police in *The Balcony*. This season: Smuggler in *The Constant Couple*, Old Bellair in *The Man of Mode*.

ROGER MICHELL *Director*
Theatre: Awarded the RSC Buzz Goodbody prize in 1977 for his production of *Bingo & Krapp's Last Tape*. For two years he was at the Royal Court, where he assisted both Beckett and Osborne and directed various plays in the Theatre Upstairs, including Mike McGrath's *The Key Tag* and Nick Darke's *The Catch*. Directing work includes *The White Glove* (Lyric, Hammersmith) and *Private Dick* (Lyric, Hammersmith and West End), both of which he co-wrote with Richard Maher, *What the Butler Saw* (Cambridge Theatre Company), *Macbeth* (Southampton), *Sexual Perversity in Chicago* (Hampstead), *Small Change* (Brighton), *The Archangel Michael* (Sheffield), *Romeo and Juliet* (Young Vic), *Happy Days*.
RSC: Assistant Director for *The Merry Wives of Windsor, The Dillen, Mary, After the Queen, Othello, Mephisto*; Director of *The Dead Monkey, Merchant of Venice* (NatWest tour), *Temptation, Hamlet* (NatWest tour), This season: *The Constant Couple*.

JAMES PUREFOY *Footman*
Theatre: Title role in *Henry V* (at Central), Romeo in *Romeo and Juliet* (Thorndike, Leatherhead), Walter in *Mary Morgan* (Riverside Studios). Alan Strang in *Equus* (Confederacy of Fools Theatre Company UK tour).
RSC: This season; Footman in *The Constant Couple*, Donalbain/Cream Faced Loon in *Macbeth*, Ferdinand in *The Tempest*. **Film:** *Eclipsed.*

STEPHEN RAYNE *Assistant Director*
Theatre: BEd Drama from London University. As an actor, seasons at Colchester, Bubble Theatre, Nottingham, Leeds, Leicester, Greenwich, Southampton and New Shakespeare Company. As assistant director work includes *The Rivals, I Have Been Here Before* (York), *Look No Hans, Who Plays Wins, Me and My Girl* (London) and *Pajama Game* (UK tour). As Director, *Yorkshire Tragedy, Twelfth Night, The Country Wife, The Room* (Drama Schools), *Mushrooms over Whitehall* (King's Head), *Moll Flanders, Can Opener* (Theatre Royal, York) *The Comedy of Errors* (York and Scandinavia), *To Have or Have Not* (Yuval, Israel), *John Bull's Other Island* (CTC), *Against Two Tides* (USA).
RSC: Assistant Director for *Kiss Me Kate, They Shoot Horses Don't They?, The Great White Hope, The Comedy of Errors* and *Hamlet* (RSC/NatWest tour 1987). As Director, *Venus and Adonis, Hero and Leander* (RSC Festival). This season: Assistant Director for *The Constant Couple*.

AMANDA ROOT *Angelica*
Theatre: Essie in *The Devil's Disciple* (Leeds Playhouse). *The Dragon's Tail* (Apollo), Adela in *The House of Bernarda Alba* (Globe).
RSC: Hermia in *A Midsummer Night's Dream*, Juliet in *Romeo and Juliet* (1983 RSC/NatWest tour and Stratford), Jessica in *The Merchant of Venice*, Moth in *Love's Labour's Lost*, Lucy in *Today*. Neuroza in *Tell Me Honestly* (Not the RSC Festival 1984/85). This season: Angelica in *The Constant Couple*, Lady Macbeth in *Macbeth*, Harriet in *The Man of Mode*.
Television: *This Lightning Always Strikes Twice, Ladies In Charge, The South Bank Show – Gothic, Jackanory, Mary Rose*. **Other:** Recently directed and produced children's pantomime for London hospitals.

JEREMY SAMS *Composer*
Theatre: Composer and Musical Director for *Ring Round the Moon, Jumpers* (Royal Exchange, Manchester), *Vanity Fair* (Cheek by Jowl), *The Blue Angel* (Liverpool Playhouse), *On the Razzle* (Leeds Playhouse), *The Scarlet Pimpernel* (Chichester and West End), *As You Like It, Edward II, The Country Wife, Don Carlos* (Royal Exchange, Manchester), *Twelfth Night* (Sheffield Crucible). Musical Director for *Carousel* (Royal Exchange), *Carmen Jones* (Sheffield Crucible).
RSC: *The Merry Wives of Windsor, Crimes in Hot Countries, Downchild, The Castle, A Midsummer Night's Dream, The Dead Monkey, The Merchant of Venice* and *Much Ado About Nothing* (RSC/NatWest tour), *Temptation, Hyde Park, Measure for Measure, Hamlet* (RSC/NatWest tour). This season: *The Constant Couple.* **Radio:** Talks and recitals on Radio 3.
Writing: Opera translations: *Johnny Strikes Up* (Opera North), *Zemire et Azor* (Camden Festival), *L'Etoile* (Guildhall School), *The Magic Flute* (ENO).

KEN SHORTER *Constable/Footman*
Theatre: Seasons at Birmingham, Nottingham, Leeds, Liverpool, Sheffield, Southampton and Cambridge including Pierre in *Blues, Whites and Reds,* Paolo Poali in *Servant of Two Masters* (and UK tour), McKenzie in *Reluctant Heroes,* Oblensky in *A Patriot for Me,* Jacques Roux in *Marat-Sade,* Ossip in *Wild Honey,* The Ballplayer in *Insignificance,* title role in *The Immortalist,* Eddie the Denims in *Leave Him to Heaven* (New London), Wolf in *Red Devil Battery Sign* (Phoenix), Greta in *Bent* (Criterion). *The Royal Hunt of the Sun, Pericles, Twelfth Night* (Prospect Theatre Company tour of UK and abroad), *Hamlet, The Rocky Horror Show* (London Theatre Company tour abroad), Biff in *Death of A Salesman,* Dorimant in *The Man of Mode,* Orlando in *As You Like It,* Valentine in *You Never Can Tell,* Victor in *Burning Bridges,* Martin Cash in *Cash.*
RSC: Officer in *The Comedy of Errors,* Bernardo/Player in *Hamlet* (RSC NatWest tour 1987). This season: Constable in *The Constant Couple,* 2nd Murderer in *Macbeth,* Boatswain in *The Tempest.*
Television: *Casualty, Rockliffe's Babies, Dick Turpin, Leave Him to Heaven, You Can't See Round Corners.* **Film:** *Stone, Dragon Slayer, Sunday Too Far Away, Maybe This Time, Ned Kelly.*

DAVID SOLOMON *Footman*
Born: Madras, India. **Trained:** Royal Academy of Dramatic Art.
Theatre: Attendant in *Women Beware Women* (Royal Court).
RSC: This season: Footman in *The Constant Couple.*

MARK SPROSTON *Clincher Junior*
Theatre: Seasons at Contact Theatre (Manchester), Haymarket Theatre (Leicester), Palace Theatre (Westcliff) including Henry IV in *Henry IV Part 1,* Barry in *Saved,* Townley in *London Cuckolds, The Devil and the Good Lord* (Lyric, Hammersmith), Jean in *Journeys Among the Dead* (Riverside Studios), *The Three Sisters* (Shared Experience and UK tour), Enobarbus in *Antony and Cleopatra* (UK tour).
RSC: Maxwell/Kid Kamm/Mario in *They Shoot Horses Don't They?* Abraham in *Romeo and Juliet,* Pressman 2 in *The Great White Hope.* This season: Clincher Junior in *The Constant Couple,* Angus/1st Murderer in *Macbeth,* Young Bellair in *The Man of Mode.*
Television: *Wrinkly.*
Film: *Sammy and Rosie Get Laid, A Hazard of Hearts.*

JILL SPURRIER *Lady Darling*
Theatre: Seasons at Lincoln, Glasgow, including Mrs Arbuthnot in *A Woman of No Importance,* Hermione Hushabye in *Heartbreak House,* Lady Markby in *An Ideal Husband,* Chinchilla in *Misia Sert,* Portia in *The Merchant of Venice,* Polina in *The Seagull* (Greenwich), Nancy in *Steaming* (Haymarket), Cariola in *The Duchess of Malfi* (UK tour). Toured Caracas, Germany, Holland and Venice with Citizen's Theatre.
RSC: The Abbess in *The Comedy of Errors, Hamlet* (RSC/NatWest tour 1987). This season: Lady Darling in *The Constant Couple,* Gentlewoman in *Macbeth.*
Television: *Within These Walls, The Magnificent One, Blood Red Noses.*
Radio: *Misia Sert.*

MELANIE THAW *Footman*
Theatre: Seasons at Manchester Royal Exchange, including Marchioness of Mondecar in *Don Carlos,* Imogen Twambley in *The Cabinet Minister.*
RSC: This season: Footman in *The Constant Couple,* Miranda in *The Tempest,* Ann in *Restoration.*

ULTZ *Designer*
Theatre: Designs in Repertory: Seasons at Glasgow Citizens', Birmingham Rep., Stratford East, Exeter. Designs for John Caird's production of *As You Like It* (Klarateatern, Stockholm), Adrian Noble's production of *Twelfth Night* (Ginza Saison Theatre, Tokyo), *The Cherry Orchard* (Stratford Ontario). As writer/director/designer in collaboration with Martin Duncan: *The Amusing Spectacle of Cinderella, A Night in Old Peking* (Lyric, Hammersmith), *Merrie Pranckes* (ICA), *All in All, Leonore!* (Sheffield Crucible) and a new adaptation of Goldoni's *The Servant of Two Masters* (Cambridge Theatre Company). As director/designer: *A Midsummer Night's Dream* at the National Arts Centre, Ottawa, *Pericles, The Taming of the Shrew* (Stratford East), *Perikles* (Stockholm's Stadsteater). Designs for the RSC: *Good* (London and Broadway), *The Twin Rivals, Naked Robots, Our Friends in the North, The Comedy of Errors, The Merchant of Venice, The Art of Success.* Designer and co-director for *Deathwatch/The Maids.* This season: *The Constant Couple, The Man of Mode.*

CLAUDETTE WILLIAMS *Tom Errand's Wife*
Theatre: *Spell No. 7* (Donmar Warehouse), Odessa in *Amen Corner,* Chorus in *Medea* (Young Vic and Theatr Clwyd). *Ending, The Four Seasons* (Edinburgh Festival). UK Tours: *Jelly Roll Soul* (Grand Union Theatre Group).
RSC: This season: Tom Errand's Wife in *The Constant Couple,* Bivoy in *The Man of Mode,* Chorus in *The Love of the Nightingale.*
Television: *Rainbow, To Have and To Hold, Fighting Back, Happy Families, Adrian Mole, The Cage.*

JOHN WOOLF *Music Director*
RSC: Music Director for *Cymbeline, Julius Caesar* (1979), *Othello* (1979), *Romeo and Juliet, King Lear, The Roaring Girl, Julius Caesar* (1983), *Twelfth Night, The Comedy of Errors, Philistines, Troilus and Cressida, The Winter's Tale, A Midsummer Night's Dream, Hyde Park, Measure for Measure.* Arranged music for *The Twin Rivals* and *Molière.* This season: Music Director for *The Constant Couple.*

Royal Shakespeare Company

Sponsored by

Royal Insurance

RSC REPERTOIRE 1988

Stratford-upon-Avon Box Office (0789) 295623

ROYAL SHAKESPEARE THEATRE

Much Ado About Nothing
by William Shakespeare

Macbeth
by William Shakespeare

The Tempest
by William Shakespeare

Henry VI/Richard III
by William Shakespeare

SWAN THEATRE

The Constant Couple
by George Farquhar

The Plain Dealer
by William Wycherley

The Man of Mode
by George Etherege

Restoration
by Edward Bond

THE OTHER PLACE

Across Oka
by Robert Holman

King John
by William Shakespeare

Supported by Hancox garden machinery

The Love of the Nightingale
by Timberlake Wertenbaker

Campesinos
by Nick Darke

London Box Office (01) 638 8891

BARBICAN THEATRE

The Jew of Malta
by Christopher Marlowe

Supported by Herald Press

Twelfth Night
by William Shakespeare

The Merchant of Venice
by William Shakespeare

Julius Caesar
by William Shakespeare

THE PIT

Cymbeline
by William Shakespeare

Fashion
by Doug Lucie

Temptation
by Václav Havel

The Revenger's Tragedy
by Cyril Tourneur

Titus Andronicus
by William Shakespeare

RSC in the West End

PALACE THEATRE
Box Office (01) 437 6834
Les Misérables
The Victor Hugo Musical

AMBASSADORS THEATRE
Box Office (01) 836 6111
Les Liaisons Dangereuses
by Christopher Hampton

SAVOY THEATRE
Box Office (01) 836 8888
Kiss Me Kate
by Cole Porter

RSC
Swan Theatre

Royal Shakespeare Company
Incorporated under Royal Charter as the
Royal Shakespeare Theatre
Patron Her Majesty the Queen
President Sir Kenneth Cork
Chairman of the Council Geoffrey A Cass
Vice Chairman Dennis L Flower
Advisory Direction Peggy Ashcroft, Peter Brook, Trevor Nunn
Artistic Director and Chief Executive Terry Hands
Direction Bill Alexander, John Barton, John Caird, Ron Daniels,
Terry Hands, Barry Kyle, Adrian Noble
Director Emeritus Trevor Nunn
Administration
John Bradley *Technical Services Administrator*
David Brierley *General Manager*
Peter Harlock *Publicity Controller*
James Langley *Production Controller*
Tim Leggatt *Planning Controller*
Genista McIntosh *Senior Administrator*
James Sargant *Barbican Administrator*
William Wilkinson *Financial Controller*
Deputies
Stephen Browning *Publicity, London*
David Fletcher *Finance*
Gillian Ingham *Publicity, Stratford*
Carol Malcolmson *Planning*

Swan Theatre
Judith Cheston *Press* (0789) 296655
Peter Cholerton *Property Master*
Mark Collins *Master Carpenter*
Sonja Dosanjh *Company Manager*
Wayne Dowdeswell *Chief Electrician*
Brian Glover *RSC Collection*
Judith Greenwood *Deputy Chief Electrician*
Josie Horton *Deputy Wardrobe Mistress*
Geoff Locker *Production Manager*
Chris Neale *House Manager*
Eileen Relph *House Manager*
Richard Rhodes *Deputy Theatre Manager*
Emma Romer *Publicity*
Graham Sawyer *Theatre Manager*
Ursula Selbiger *Box Office Manager*
Michael Tubbs *Music Director*

Production Credits for The Constant Couple
Scenery, painting, properties, costumes and wigs made in RST
Workshops, Stratford-upon-Avon. Swan Property Manager Mark
Graham.

Facilities
In addition to bar and coffee facilities on the ground floor, there is
wine on sale on the first floor bridge outside Gallery 1. Toilets,
including facilities for disabled people, are situated on the ground
floor only.

RSC Collection
Over a thousand items on view: costumes, props, pictures and
sound recordings illustrating the changes in staging from medi-
eval times to the use of the thrust stage in the Swan, and
comparisons of past productions of the current season's plays.
Come and see our exhibition; browse in the sales and refreshments
area – and book a backstage tour. Open weekdays from 9.15 am.
Sundays from 12.00.

'The Constant Couple': a Critical Commentary

by Simon Trussler

The Compiler

Simon Trussler has contributed the commentaries to eight previous volumes in Methuen's Swan Theatre Plays series. He has been an editor of *New Theatre Quarterly* and its predecessor *Theatre Quarterly* since 1971, and presently teaches in the Drama Department of Goldsmiths' College, University of London. *Shakespearean Concepts*, due from Methuen London in 1989, will be the latest of nearly two-dozen books on theatrical subjects he has written or edited, and he was also the founding-editor of the Royal Shakespeare Company's *Yearbook* in 1978, compiling the annual editions until 1985.

> Let fall no words that may offend the Fair;
> Observe Decorums, dress thy Thoughts with Air;
> Go — lay the Plot, which Virtue shall adorn:
> Thus spoke the Muse; and thus didst Thou perform
> Thy *Constant Couple* does our Fame return,
> And shews our Sex can love when yours esteem,
> And *Wild-Air's* Character does plainly shew,
> A man of sense may dress and be a Beau.
> In Vizor many may their picture find;
> A pious Out-side, but a poisonous Mind.
> Religious Hypocrites thou'st open laid,
> Those holy Cheats by which our Isle is sway'd.
> Oh! mayst thou live! And Dryden's Place supply,
> So long till thy best Friends shall bid thee die;
> Could I from bounteous Heav'n one wish obtain,
> I'd make thy person lasting as thy Fame.
>   *Susannah Centlivre (1667-1723)*

Stage History

The Constant Couple was an outstanding success on its first production by the Drury Lane company on 28 November 1699, and reputedly achieved the then astonishing total of 53 performances in its first season (and, it was claimed, a further 23 in Dublin). Farquhar's friend and mentor Robert Wilks, himself fresh from Ireland, played Sir Harry Wildair, and Susannah Verbruggen took the part of Lady Lurewell. One of the leading actors from the old company, George Powell, played Colonel Standard, but seems to have been outshone by another of Farquhar's acquaintances from Dublin, Henry Norris, who was thereafter known as 'Jubilee Dicky' from his success in this relatively minor role. The Clinchers were the comedians Pinkethman and Bullock, and the veteran comic actor Joe Haines took the part of Tom Errand.

The Constant Couple entered the regular repertoire of Drury Lane, with Wilks a reliable draw as Sir Harry, and Farquhar's protégée Anne Oldfield taking over the role of Lurewell after Mrs. Verbruggen's death in 1703. A measure of the play's popularity was its regular choice for benefit performances, when sure-fire box-office success was the main criterion: Lacy Ryan thus played Wildair for his own benefit at Lincoln's Inn Fields in 1731, with James Quin as Standard, and Henry Giffard chose the part for his return to the stage at Drury Lane in 1739 in a benefit for his wife, who played Lurewell, with Macklin as Clincher Senior. Peg Woffington, having taken the town by storm as Silvia in *The Recruiting Officer* upon her first appearance at Covent Garden in 1740, went on to make Sir Harry in *The Constant Couple* a 'breeches part', and for her own benefit in 1743 appeared as Lurewell, opposite the Wildair of David Garrick and the Angelica of Kitty Clive. Although later Wildairs included Harry Woodward, the great pantomime player, in 1749, and 'Gentleman' O'Brien in 1762, both at Drury Lane, it was now firmly established as a 'breeches part', and when Lowndes published an edition in 1791 giving the cast-lists for Drury Lane, Covent Garden, and the Haymarket, Wildair was assigned to Mrs. Jordan, Mrs. Achment, and Mrs. Goodall respectively.

Although revivals continued into the nineteenth century, the play lost favour, presumably for its lack of Victorian virtues, until its revival in our own century under the direction of Alec Clunes at the Arts Theatre in July 1943. In the actor-manager tradition, Clunes himself played Wildair, as he did again in later revivals at the Arts in September 1945 and at the Winter Garden in March 1952. The most recent London production, directed by Richard Cottrell, opened at the New Theatre in June 1967, with Robert Hardy as Sir Harry, Helen Lindsay as Lurewell, and Timothy West as Smuggler.

George Farquhar: a Brief Chronology

1677 *c.* Born in Londonderry, son of an impoverished Church of England clergyman.

1689 Presumably still in Londonderry during the Jacobite siege of the city from April to July (and claimed by his mother to have fought in the Battle of the Boyne in 1690).

1694 Entered Trinity College, Dublin, as a 'sizar' — receiving scant board and tuition in return for menial duties.

1696 Left Trinity College without his degree, and acted (indifferently, by all accounts) at the Smock Alley Theatre in Dublin, making his debut as Othello.

1697 Accidentally wounded another actor in a stage duel, and, apparently on the advice of his friend and fellow-actor Robert Wilks, left for London to try his fortune as a playwright.

1698 His first play, the comedy *Love and a Bottle* (published 1699), performed with moderate success at Drury Lane in December, and his anecdotal novella, *Adventures of Covent-Garden*, published anonymously in the same month.

1699 First performance of *The Constant Couple; or, a Trip to the Jubilee* (published 1700) at Drury Lane in November. Credited with the 'discovery' of Anne Oldfield in the Mitre tavern.

1700 Contributed to a published collection of *Familiar and Courtly Letters*.

1701 *Sir Harry Wildair* the unsuccessful sequel to *The Constant Couple*, performed at Drury Lane in April, and published. Contributed to *Letters of Wit, Politicks, and Morality*.

1702 His adaptation of Fletcher's *The Wild Goose Chase* as *The Inconstant* (published 1702) performed at Drury Lane without much success, just before the closing of the theatres for six weeks following the death of William III in March. The satirical comedy *The Twin-Rivals* (published 1703) followed in December, also at Drury Lane, and was an even more pronounced failure. His miscellany of occasional verse and letters, *Love and Business*, published, including the epistolary 'Discourse upon Comedy'.

1703 Marriage to Margaret Pemell, a widow with three children, whose poverty apparently surprised him. The short farce *The Stage-Coach* (published 1704), adapted from the French, performed at Lincoln's Inn Fields in December, or January 1704, and became an extremely popular afterpiece.

1704 Commissioned as a Lieutenant of Grenadiers, securing him a small but reliable income of £54 a year. Received almost £100 from a Dublin benefit performance of *The Constant Couple*. Birth of his first daughter, Anne Marguerite.

1705 On recruiting service in Lichfield and Shrewsbury. Birth of his second daughter, Mary.

1706 *The Recruiting Officer* (set in Shrewsbury) performed successfully at Drury Lane in April and published. Well received, but Farquhar was already ill, presumably with tuberculosis, and may have sold his commission to raise money.

1707 *The Beaux Stratagem* (set in Lichfield) performed at the new theatre in the Haymarket in March, and published. But Farquhar now gravely ill, and he died in a 'back garret' in St. Martin's Lane in April or May, in his thirtieth year. The funeral was paid for by Wilks, to whom Farquhar entrusted the care of his 'two helpless girls'. Posthumous publication of the unauthorized *Love's Catechism* (largely derived from *The Beaux Stratagem*) and of the heroic poem *Barcellona*.

A Context for 'The Constant Couple'

George Farquhar has suffered from critical neglect largely, it seems, because he won't quite 'fit'. His near contemporaries Congreve and Vanbrugh, though they both outlived him by some twenty years, can be seen as developing a dramatic tradition begun by Dryden, Etherege, and Wycherley: but Farquhar is much more distinctively his own man. 'Restoration comedy', it is now generally recognized, simply will not do as a catch-all for the work of this writer, whose spiritual as well as chronological home bridges the seventeenth and eighteenth centuries, yet who can be 'placed' no more appositely among the Augustans. There he sits, encusped in solitary splendour, between a long-declining Age of Aquarius and an ascendant Age of Reason.

Barely twenty when he wrote his first play, *Love and a Bottle*, Farquhar could not yet quite afford or perhaps did not quite know how to manage an entirely personal mode. He has even been charged with mixing titillation and moralizing after the manner of Cibber's earlier *Love's Last Shift*, in contrasting his riotous rake with the 'sober and modest' brother of his mistress, and, of course, rewarding them both with wealthy brides (not to mention employing the 'bed-trick' to regularize the climactic matches). Yet the energy of the play lies not in its drift towards marriage, but in the almost Jonsonian range of eccentrics who flesh out 'the varieties of the town' — the fop Mockmode, the poet Lyrick and his long-suffering landlady Mrs. Bullfinch, the bookseller Pamphlet, the dancing-master Rigadoon and the fencing-master

Nimblewrist, not to mention the hapless whore Trudge, amongst all of whom the madcap Irish hero Roebuck wanders like a would-be experienced innocent at large. Farquhar's biographer Willard Connely notes the careful casting of the Drury Lane production of 1698, and suggests that 'it is as if Farquhar had intently studied the work of the entire cast' of Vanbrugh's recent hit *The Relapse*, 'and built his own play around the talents of the lot': certainly, such an idea becomes all the more interesting if one compares the *use* Farquhar made of those talents — even to having Joe Haines write a Prologue to be spoken by the womanizing tippler George Powell, the play's title made flesh.

Although infrequently revived, *Love and a Bottle* had a successful enough initial run to gain its author two benefits, enabling him to live a little more comfortably while he wrote *The Constant Couple* — but Farquhar evidently rested a little too long on the income and the laurels from this, the triumphant success of the season of 1699. It took him another eighteen months to come up with *Sir Harry Wildair*, which suffered the fate of most sequels — though it managed a respectable first run, presumably on the strength of public curiosity to see how all the familiar characters were making out after marriage. Predictably, Sir Harry has suffered a relapse, admittedly under the impression that Angelica is dead, while marriage has brought out only the worst in Standard and Lurewell. The plotting — never Farquhar's strongest point — here has to bear an undue share of the weight, and finally collapses under the bathetic stress of a disguised Angelica revealing herself as her own ghost.

His next play, *The Inconstant*, partially resolved Farquhar's problem with plots by taking over an existing one, from Fletcher's late Jacobean comedy *The Wild Goose Chase*, and somewhat simplifying its last two acts. The play survived to its sixth night, and was revived with some success later in the century, but for the moment the death of the king in March 1702 eclipsed its own and Farquhar's fortunes, and he set to work quickly on *The Twin-Rivals*, which had its first night in December of the same year. Subsequent criticism has been largely shaped by the need to account for the play's initial failure — which, one suspects, was due not to its relatively high moral tone (now becoming acceptable if dressed-up in sentiment), but to its formal originality, in portraying unalleviated vice as vicious yet still a proper subject for comedy. Certainly, the RSC revival in 1982 — the first, apparently, for nearly two hundred years — demonstrated both the sheer theatricality of the piece, and its resolute nonconformity to pattern.

It is also, for Farquhar, very tightly plotted, around a younger brother's attempt to defraud his marginally older twin out of his inheritance. Sex here not only comes an acknowledged second to money, but, as mediated in the character of Mandrake the midwife and bawd, is rather more closely connected with childbirth than theatrical convention expected, one of the characters actually suffering an illegitimate though offstage pregnancy. There is, not unsurprisingly, more dramatic energy in the fraudulent lordling's demonstration of his unworthiness than in his eventual exposure, but both the energy and the emphasis are Jonsonian — as, indeed, was Farquhar's defence of the play in its published preface. If it has not quite caught the tone of voice in which to be 'seriously funny', it strikes out in a remarkable new direction which Farquhar was shortly to follow through in *The Recruiting Officer* and *The Beaux Stratagem*.

In between, the short farce *The Stage-Coach* — dealing with the 'mistakes of a night', as true love blossoms in the attempt to save a girl from her guardian's preferred suitor — also anticipated Farquhar's last two plays, in its country setting of an inn. As Eric Rothstein says, 'it makes one hungry for the work he did not do' between its production late in 1703 and 1706. On the other hand, it was no doubt precisely Farquhar's escape from the incestuous world of literary and theatrical London during the intervening years that tempered his final plays with the hard edge of experience — his military duties, of course, providing a background for *The Recruiting Officer*, and his own unfortunate marriage a deep-felt source for his portrayal of sexual incompatibility in *The Beaux Stratagem*. These works need no defence from me, though it's worth noting how long both were revived as rather special kinds of Restoration comedy until, ironically, a foreigner, Bertolt Brecht, recognized the stronger stuff of which *The Recruiting Officer* was made (in his own updated version, *Drums and Trumpets),* and the director Bill Gaskill brought out the full range of the socially-critical comedy of both plays in his National Theatre productions of the nineteen sixties. Summing up his own feelings about Farquhar, Gaskill said at the time that, by comparison with Dryden or even Congreve, 'he seems a very grown-up person' — and so he does, even though, as *The Beaux Stratagem* entered its third triumphant month of performances at Drury Lane in 1707, its author lay dead in a back-garret at the age of twenty-nine.

Farquhar and the War of the Theatres

Farquhar's 'New Prologue' to *The Constant Couple* is addressed to his erstwhile 'very good friend, Mr. Oldmixon, who, having two plays damn'd at the Old House, had a mind to curry favour, to have a third damn'd at the New'. The Old House was Drury Lane, as rebuilt by Wren in 1674, while the New was in fact considerably older — the converted tennis-court in Lincoln's Inn Fields, first used as a theatre in 1662 by one of the two companies granted letters patent after the Restoration of Charles II. These had joined forces in 1682, and London's theatregoers were for thirteen years served by the Drury Lane company alone, until the leading actor of his generation, Thomas Betterton, took a group of players back to Lincoln's Inn in 1695, having quarrelled with the manager at Drury Lane, the overbearing and underpaying Christopher Rich.

The 'warfare' which ensued between these two theatres was already in full swing when Farquhar's first play, *Love and a Bottle*, was staged in December 1698. But it seemed as if Farquhar, in entrusting the play to Drury Lane, might be on the losing side, for Betterton had taken with him to Lincoln's Inn Fields the best-known players of the day, including the leading actresses Elizabeth Barry and Anne Bracegirdle — and the opening production there, of Congreve's *Love for Love*, set a sparkling standard. But Drury Lane enjoyed the advantages as well as the inexperience of youth — besides a far superior theatre — and by 1699, while all the great names at Lincoln's Inn were past or passing their prime, Drury Lane was attracting the luminaries of the new generation. Susannah Verbruggen, William Pinkethman, and the young Colley Cibber had remained loyal, and over the next few years William Bullock, Farquhar's friends Robert Wilks and Henry Norris, and his protégée Anne Oldfield all joined the company. As Cibber put it in his *Apology*, 'Betterton's people . . . were most of them too far advanc'd in years to mend; and tho' we, in Drury Lane, were too young to be excellent, we were not too old to be better'. Cibber's own *Love's Last Shift* was the outstanding success in 1696 at Drury Lane, to be followed by Vanbrugh's comic sequel, *The Relapse*, in 1697, while Farquhar's achievement of over fifty performances of *The Constant Couple* in the first season alone set the seal on the young company's slow but sure ascendancy.

Farquhar remained loyal to Drury Lane until a number of its best actors, weary as much of Rich's manner as of his management, defected in the autumn of 1706 to Vanbrugh's new Queen's Theatre in the Haymarket, where Betterton's company had been in residence since its opening in the previous year. Farquhar contributed a prologue to the first production of the new season at the Queen's, in October 1706, and it was here, of course, that his last play, *The Beaux Stratagem*, opened in the following March. In the event, this was to be one of the very few successes at a playhouse whose acoustics made it unsuitable for the spoken drama. By 1708, it was given over to opera, and the actors returned to Drury Lane, where after a few further vicissitudes a new management, now including Cibber and Farquhar's friend Robert Wilks, inaugurated a period of relative stability and financial prosperity, albeit creative sterility, at the 'Old House'.

But by then, of course, Farquhar was dead, the period of active warfare having almost exactly coincided with his own brief theatrical career — and witnessed not only his own comedies, but all those of Vanbrugh, the greatest of Congreve's, and the most significant work of Cibber and Steele. The audience for them was, by comparison with Elizabethan times, still small, but its tastes and probably its social composition were changing — in ways which remain the inflammable stuff of critical debate, among both theatre and social historians. One of the very few verifiable facts is, simply, that a new, much younger generation of actors was getting into its stride, and performing the work of an equally young generation of dramatists. Although Vanbrugh had just reached his thirties, Congreve and Farquhar were both in their very early twenties when they first found theatrical success — and Wilks, when he played Farquhar's Sir Harry Wildair, was just half the age of Betterton, who was turning sixty when he created the part of 'young' Valentine in *Love for Love*.

So the change in the theatrical climate that undoubtedly did occur around the turn of the century may be partially attributed to this natural and inevitable transfer of theatrical power, as the 'first generation' of Restoration players drew near to retirement, or to death in harness. But partially, too, it was due to a change in the pervasive social mood, and this, though difficult to pin down in other ways, was very precisely pinned down so far as the theatre was concerned in the year of Farquhar's own first play by an Anglican clergyman called Jeremy Collier.

The Wits, the Cits, and Jeremy Collier

When Alderman Smuggler confronts his erstwhile apprentice Clincher in Newgate as *The Constant Couple* draws to its close, and berates him for his vicious habits, playgoing is chief among them. 'I gave an honest gentleman five guineas myself towards writing a book against it: and it has done no good, we see.' The honest gentleman was doubtless Jeremy Collier: and from the point of view of Smuggler's nonconformist friends in the City, it was a matter of lively and continuing debate whether or not his book had done any good.

The theatre had belatedly benefited from its closure during the Civil Wars and the Commonwealth, since attacks on it were tainted with a puritanism which, after the Restoration, could be perceived as tantamount to treachery. But Jeremy Collier — whose *Short View of the Immorality and Profaneness of the English Stage* had been published in 1698, and struck an immediate chord — was a High Anglican: and, so far from being of puritanical leanings, he had just absolved two traitors executed for their part in a Jacobite plot to overturn the 'glorious revolution' of 1688, which had subjected even the respectable protestantism of William and Mary to the power of parliament.

Collier's attack was not by any means the first upon a stage whose audiences and playwrights alike seemed lingeringly nostalgic for the permissive climate of the Charles II's reign. Now, the issue had become inextricably related to class; and so far as the theatre was concerned, the bourgeois 'cits' were best contained by portraying them as hypocrites, either given to the inherent selfishness which, in our play, Vizard finds vindicated by his reading of Hobbes, or to the unpatriotic duplicity by which Smuggler conducts his business. The 'work ethic' was so closely associated with Calvinistic beliefs that it was possible to sustain the attack on puritanical 'cits' even though middle-class values were lapping ever closer to the centres of political power, as they had already overwhelmed the economic. Jeremy Collier, then, had the great advantage of speaking for the middle classes, although in social status and in religious orthodoxy he remained distanced from them.

The *Short View* — which was actually of considerable length — attacked the stage both on specific and general grounds. In the first part of the book, Collier gave chapter and verse for his charges that the theatre was immodest and obscene, that it ridiculed the clergy, and that it not only portrayed vicious persons as its heroes but rewarded them, in violation of poetical justice — whose desirable extension from tragedy to comedy Collier did not invent, but to which he did give general currency. It was in the second part of the *Short View* that, citing authorities ancient and modern, Collier mounted an attack on the theatre as such, entirely justifying his opponents' charges that, while posing as a reformer of the stage, he was actually allied to the puritans in seeking to destroy it. But the scores of 'amendments' and 'answers' which poured from the presses in the wake of the *Short View* (amongst no fewer 'defences' and 'vindications' in its support) shared the disadvantage that Collier had dictated the terms of the debate, and that, in those terms, most plays of the time were very difficult indeed to defend. It is not true that the stage immediately 'reformed' itself: to the extent that tastes were changing anyway, that supreme theatrical pragmatist Colley Cibber had already anticipated the change as early as 1696, by tempering his *Love's Last Shift*, which was 'lewd for above four acts', with a highly moral conclusion. And the prologues and epilogues of the period following Collier's attack were perhaps better advised than the printed polemics in subjecting him to ridicule rather than attempting repudiation. But the *Short View* can, in the longer view, be seen as a watershed: slowly, plays as well as tastes did change, giving rise both to those singularly unfunny 'sentimental comedies' and, more interestingly, to the formal and thematic extensions of comic range attempted by John Gay and Henry Fielding.

By the end of his own career, Farquhar was writing a new kind of play which, so far from compromising his artistic integrity by responding to the external attacks, was an expression of the experiential difference between his own life and assumptions and those of a Wycherley, or of a contemporary such as Congreve. But his very earliest work, *Love and a Bottle*, had emulated Cibber's fifth-act reformation, while Collier could scarcely have welcomed such elements of *The Constant Couple* as Sir Harry's careless assumption that Angelica is a whore, and his no less careless attitude towards marriage as a means of making amends — not to mention his antics as a merry-widower in the play's eponymous sequel. When Farquhar attempted his own, indirect response to Collier in the 'Discourse upon Comedy', a Horatian epistle published in 1702, he looked to Aesop rather than Aristotle for precedent, defining comedy as 'no more at present than a well-framed tale handsomely told as an agreeable vehicle for counsel or reproof'. And he wryly acknowledged that, of all the arts and sciences, 'poetry alone, and chiefly the drama, lies open to the insults of all pretenders'. It had certainly been open, wide open, to Collier's.

The City End and the Court End

Sir Harry Wildair sends out his footmen with wedding invitations in three directions — 'you to Westminster, you to St. James's, and you into the City'. He has friends, in short, 'in town', at court, and within the 'square mile' governed by Alderman Smuggler and his fellow members of the Common Council. So far as country cousins were concerned, all three merged into that sprawling metropolitan mass which was London; but nice divisions of status, behaviour, and financial situation separated their inhabitants — divisions which had been stressed and heightened by the extreme class-consciousness of the theatre in the early Restoration period.

Despite the immense wealth and relative autonomy of the City of London, the sources of that wealth in trade and business made it, simply, ungentlemanly — since a gentleman derived his income from his land, and spent it on his leisure. Even those citizens who possessed land — which became perhaps all the more strongly the symbolic measure of wealth as it gradually ceased to be so in actuality — were, sometimes correctly, suspected of gaining it from the forfeitures imposed under Cromwell, and so of dispossessing its 'rightful' owners. (As Vizard, with unwonted honesty, says to Standard, 'Why, in the City end o' th' town we 're playing the knave to get estates', to which Standard no less frankly responds, 'And in the Court end, playing the fool in spending 'em'.) It was, of course, also from the City that the puritans had drawn much of their support, and the mercantile community remained of nonconformist inclination, not least in regarding working for their livings not just as permissible but actually desirable. With Alderman Smuggler and Vizard as its representatives, and Clincher Senior exemplifying the gauche behaviour of the newly-rich, the hostility of 'the town' towards 'the city' is still much in evidence in *The Constant Couple*, though from the scant information available it appears that the bourgeoisie were already attending the theatres in greater numbers, and by mid-century had become dominant not only among its audiences but in shaping its morality — or rather, too often, its mere moralizing.

Farquhar, of course, was new to London when he wrote *The Constant Couple*, and the play's settings and 'local colour' do not venture far from the fashionable parts of the West End, whose spinal cord was at that time still the Strand. To its south lay the 'shopping precinct', as we should now describe it, of the New Exchange (so-called to distinguish it from the Royal Exchange in the City, where merchants such as Smuggler conducted their business), and it is to the Princess's chocolate house here that Sir Harry takes Vizard to write his introduction to Angelica. To the north of the Strand stood the recently-developed Covent Garden, from which ran eastwards, then as now, Russell Street, where Wildair and Clincher are discovered in Act III, in the very shadow of Wren's Drury Lane. And it is in the enclosing piazza of Covent Garden that Wildair and Standard meet at the beginning of Farquhar's fourth act — almost as fashionable a strolling-place as 'The Park' (St. James's Park, that is) in which he opens the play. Here stood the royal palace on which courtly activity was now centered, as Whitehall began to succumb to the state bureaucracy with which it has remained synonymous.

Although Lady Lurewell lives 'in Pall Mall near the Holy Lamb' there was little development to its west, or indeed to the north, where the Haymarket was not yet even paved — its undeveloped neighbourhood being one of the reasons for the relative neglect of Vanbrugh's new theatre there, though by the 1730s it found itself in the heart of the encroaching West End. The one other specific setting for a scene in our play is, of course, Newgate Prison, in Old Bailey, which derived its name from its location at one of the two western entrances through the old city walls. Here were incarcerated the felons and debtors of the City of London and County of Middlesex — this latter including Westminster and other western suburbs, since there was to be no County of London until 1888, despite moves in that direction by Charles I in 1636. Westminster itself enjoyed no such independence as the City of London, and shared the designation of 'city' solely by virtue of its abbey church. But the presence within its expanding boundaries of parliament, royal palaces, and the law courts had ensured that the 'twin-sister cities joined by one street', as Thomas Heywood described London and Westminster in 1635, had by 1699 swelled to a continuously built-up area from beyond Wapping in the east to St. James's in the west.

Cash and Class — or 'Pounds per Annum'

No less precisely than Jane Austen, Farquhar measures out his characters' lives according to their incomes. And, in every case, their wealth is put into words from their own mouths, as if new-fangled bank-notes were now to be emblazoned on armorial bearings. Clincher thus shields himself from Tom Errand with the assertion, 'Sir, you can't master me, for I'm twenty thousand strong', and Wildair similarly feels 'a man of eight thousand pounds per annum' should be secure from all vexation. And it is Lady Lurewell herself, not one of her calculating suitors, who informs us that she is 'sole heiress and executrix to three thousand pounds a year'.

Money is no less significant in its absence. Colonel Standard, disbanded with his regiment, recognizes that no amount of gallantry can make up for his impoverishment — a highly topical issue, this, since it was as recently as February 1699 that the Disbanding Act, passed at the behest of a predominantly Tory ministry, had halved the army to seven thousand men, much against the wishes of the king. And Lady Darling is curiously silent about Angelica's fortune or lack of it: falling back on the family tree, she declares to Sir Harry that her family's blood 'for many generations has run in the purest channel of unsullied honour'.

An economic subtext underlies the whole of Farquhar's action. He quickly lets it be known of Colonel Standard that 'my father's a lord, and my elder brother a beau': so the gallant officer's poverty is due not just to his disbandment, but to the effects of primogeniture — the inheritance of the whole of an estate by the first-born son. As a benefactor of the system, Clincher Senior duly delights in his own father's death, and Clincher Junior anticipates his brother's no less eagerly — while the elder son's abortive apprenticeship suggests the origins of his father's fortune in work rather than in possession of land. For, as Sir Harry recognizes with or without irony, a gentleman is distinguished precisely by his unalleviated leisure. Wildair thus reacts with unfeigned shock to Lurewell's accusation of dishonour in his business dealings — 'Why, madam, I never had any business in my life' — and later, declining to defend his honour in a duel with Standard, his catalogue of genteel attributes begins and ends with the ability to 'dance, sing, ride, fence, understand the languages'. Accused of cowardice, he claims that his wealth precludes it: 'Coward, sir! I have eight thousand pounds a year, sir.'

And class, in the end, closes its ranks against 'mere' wealth. The social origins of Clincher — his father no doubt an honest yeoman, who 'broke his neck a fox-hunting' — confirm that he is no better able to make 'genteel' use of his wealth for leisure than Smuggler may be assumed to employ his own riches honestly in business. And while Lurewell's breeding somehow protects her from the taint of Smuggler's illicit dealings (upon which she is nonetheless obscurely dependent), Clincher, Smuggler, and Vizard end the play at best discountenanced — and at worst disinherited.

The Bank of England, it is relevant to note, had been founded as recently as 1694. Thus was born the economic life-lie of the National Debt, in the Bank's legal entitlement to issue paper money and so to raise further funds by recycling capital already 'loaned' to the government. The Goldsmiths' Company, with a vested interest in more traditional forms of security, had tried to break the Bank in 1697 by demanding payment upon an amount assembled in notes they knew to be in excess of its 'real' reserves: but the government intervened to prevent it. Wealth, for so long measured in the possession of land or at least in material goods, could now quite literally and securely be amassed in pieces of paper.

So there is a raw truth behind the game of 'buss and guinea' in which Smuggler wants Lurewell to join. The old boundaries are beginning to blur. For all her vaunted fortune, Lurewell has evidently been trying to enhance it by investing in Smuggler's schemes, and although the conventions of comedy can rescue her from his clutches, the conventions of the new economics were not always to prove so kind. Nor, for that matter, were the conventions of the new drama. Barely thirty years later, the no less immediate success of another play at Drury Lane was based in part on its inversion of Farquhar's typology, showing how a scheming, man-despising woman could corrupt an otherwise honest apprentice, much to the distress of his incorruptibly honest employer — Alderman Smuggler made good, as George Lillo's eponymous hero of *The London Merchant*.

Writers and Critics on Farquhar

Farquhar's chief characters are also adventurers, but they are of a romantic, not a knavish stamp, and succeed no less by their honesty than by their boldness. . . . They are real gentlemen and only pretended impostors. Vanbrugh's upstart lover . . . we have little sympathy for . . . and no respect at all. But we have every sort of goodwill towards Farquhar's heroes, who have as many peccadillos to answer for, and play as many rogue's tricks, but are honest fellows at bottom.

William Hazlitt (1819)

Of the four [Restoration] dramatists of whom we have endeavoured to give some account . . . Farquhar had the highest animal spirits, with fits of the deepest sympathy, the greatest wish to please rather than strike, the most agreeable diversity of character, the best instinct in avoiding the revolting extravagances of the time, and the happiest invention in plot and situation, and, therefore, is to be pronounced, upon the whole, the finest dramatic genius, and the most likely to be of lasting popularity.

Leigh Hunt (1840)

But in known images of life I guess
The labour greater, and th' indulgence less.
Observe how seldom ev'n the best succeed:
Tell me if Congreve's fools are fools indeed?
What pert low dialogue has Farqu'ar writ!
How Van wants grace, who never wanted wit!

Alexander Pope (1737)

It is too low for criticism; it is too bad to dwell upon. . . . If I saw anything in [The Constant Couple] to commend, I would readily and gladly point it out; but it appears to me to be altogether, and in every particular, so destitute of merit that . . . I shall never, by my own choice, read it again.

Richard Cumberland (1817)

He lies even further from literature than Vanbrugh, but he has a greater knowledge of life.

Edmund Gosse (1891)

In [Congreve's] plays especially, but also in those of Wycherley and Vanbrugh, we have a constant sense of frequenting a small coterie of exceedingly disagreeable people. Their talk is essentially coterie-talk, keyed up to the pitch of a particular and narrow set. It is Farquhar's great merit to have released comedy from this circle of malign enchantment. Even in *The Constant Couple* and *Sir Harry Wildair* his characters have not quite the coterie stamp. We feel, at any rate, that they are studied from an outside point of view, by one who does not mistake the conventions of the coterie for laws of nature.

William Archer (1906)

We do not try to compare a hollyhock with a tulip, and it is just as absurd to compare the work of George Farquhar with the bulk of Restoration comedy. . . . Farquhar, it is true, commented upon manners, but such criticism was only a side issue with him. He was more intent upon lively action and the telling of a roguish tale. . . . Life was a discoloured and painful thing to him, and the only remedy was to treat it as a game, not the delicate intellectual game of Etherege, but a good Elizabethan romp.

Bonamy Dobrée (1924)

A supreme complacency, a point-blank refusal to be discomfited, and an affection for the tippler's leer are all part and parcel of Harry Wildair. Theatrical 'lifemanship' can seldom have been more persuasively expounded.

Kenneth Tynan (1952)

He includes military characters in nearly all of his plays, and through them provides comment . . . on England's changing diplomatic and military position. He makes a soldier's matter-of-fact evaluations of international affairs, and only rarely is he chauvinistic. The topicality of his plays . . . makes a strong claim on the historical imagination and is, I believe, pure gain. But it frequently crowds out extended treatment of social issues.

John Loftis (1959)

If he had not died young, Farquhar would presumably have kept on writing, since he, unlike his most famous predecessors and contemporaries . . . depended upon his pen for a living. How his work would have developed, what part he would have played in the literary culture of England, we cannot know. We can only wish that we and he had been given the chance to find out.

Eric Rothstein (1967)

The Pocket-Book of Alderman Smuggler

If the inter-war period in our own century was a 'long weekend', the years which saw the seventeenth century become the eighteenth encompassed a very short weekend indeed — between the Treaty of Ryswick which ended the Augsburg wars in September 1697, and the outbreak of the War of the Spanish Succession in May 1702. The enemy, in both dynastic conflicts, was France — and hence the particular obloquy attached to Smuggler for importing 'French wines in Spanish casks'.

In *The Constant Couple*, both Wildair and Standard have fought in the Netherlands, the main battleground of the Augsburg wars, and despite his disbandment Standard anticipates early recall: for, as Sir Harry puts it, 'treaties made in France are never kept'. Admittedly, he is here referring to an amorous rather than a military cease-fire, but it appears that other kinds of honour are also subject to a sea-change — for Sir Harry frankly admits that while he is happy to duel with a mere French beau, accepting Standard's challenge in London would be 'downright madness'. Even his reluctant agreement to marry Angelica is made to appear as much a matter of cowardice as of frustrated desire — though here it is not so much fear of his adversary as of the consequences of murdering him, for, as he has earlier been told (ironically, by Vizard himself), a 'Middlesex jury' would hang him 'purely because you're a gentleman'. So much for honour: as for love, Sir Harry spends much of his time in *The Constant Couple* either making a fool of himself in Angelica's eyes, or being made a fool of in Lady Lurewell's. And 'love and honour' were not merely words engraved on the ring that Standard gave to Lurewell twelve long years ago, but the criteria by which the late seventeenth century judged its 'heroic' characters.

Even the gallant Colonel Standard, whose capacity for issuing challenges becomes almost a humour, is for most of the action somebody else's dupe. Indeed, it is possible to read the two-part title of the play as an ironic reminder that *The Constant Couple* are no nearer to being truly constant than the *Trip to the Jubilee* is to being undertaken. 'A great many quarrel at *The Trip to the Jubilee* for a misnomer', confessed Farquhar in his 'Preface to the Reader' of the printed text; and he continued, 'I must tell them, that perhaps there are greater trips in this play' — presumably intending a pun on the alternative sense of 'trip' as a blunder, accident, or mistake. If Rome — where the celebrations for the papal jubilee were due to begin on Christmas Eve 1699 — does begin to take on the almost metaphysical quality of Pinter's Sidcup in *The Caretaker*, as an entirely unattainable destination, so too is constancy between any couple made to appear an impossible goal. Standard's pursuit of Lurewell, in ignorance of her real identity, disqualifies him *tout court*, while Lurewell's circus of admirers prance to the tune of her misandry rather than

to strains of unrequited love. Wildair and Standard achieve happy endings by pure accident, but Lurewell wins either way: in her guerrilla warfare against every eligible male in the play, or by the treaty which brings that war to a close — a treaty which, as the play's sequel confirms, will prove as temporary as the Treaty of Ryswick which had just 'ended' the war against the French.

My impression of a somewhat incompetent and ultimately tame Wildair is offered at least as a corrective to the familiar view that he is a sort of jovial persona for his creator, or to Eric Rothstein's more recent description of him as an *honnête homme* who is 'the central organizing agent' of the play. Now, quite apart from Wildair's demonstrable inability to organize a rice pudding, even at the structural level his centrality is limited to linking the Lurewell and Angelica halves of the plot — a dubious honour he shares with Vizard, who does a good deal of organizing of his own, some of it quite successful, until he overreaches himself by being indiscreetly confessional while making lustful advances to his own transvestite uncle. But if Smuggler is Vizard's uncle, he too is related to Angelica, as also apparently are the Clinchers . . . a case, one suspects, of an ancient but impoverished family making judicious alliances with (and so legitimizing) the newly-rich. No wonder that Wildair, who has a baronetcy as well as that eight thousand a year, is a catch worth the sinking of a mother's pride.

Farquhar, without becoming overtly didactic, thus recognizes the economic realities of late seventeenth-century life. His Wildair is able to remain an amiable but ineffective man-about-town thanks to his inherited income, while all around him the Clinchers and the Smugglers display — in 'real life' with considerably more success — the power of the newly-rich to win their way to status as well as wealth. And the 'family tree' of *The Constant Couple* is less overtly stressed but no less significant than all those complicated interrelationships in Congreve's *The Way of the World*. But the hero of the play is not Wildair, or constancy, or even — though she has a better claim than any of the men to the title — the Lady Lurewell, whose real name turns out, with a nod in the direction of the misanthropic hero of Wycherley's *The Plain Dealer*, to be Manly. No: if there is a hero — and if it is not a hero, it is surely the 'central organizing agent' — it is that well-stuffed pocket-book of Alderman Smuggler's.

For Further Reading

A critical edition of Farquhar's *Works*, edited by Shirley Strum Kenny, is to be published in 1988 by Oxford University Press. This will be the first full edition since the two-volume *Complete Works* edited by Charles Stonehill (London: Nonesuch Press, 1930; reprinted, New York: Gordian Press, 1967), which is handsome, though its annotations are not invariably reliable. The Mermaid selection edited by William Archer (London: Unwin, 1906) is still widely available in reprint, and includes *The Constant Couple* and *The Twin-Rivals* as well as *The Recruiting Officer* and *The Beaux Stratagem*. These two masterpieces may also be found in Louis A. Strauss's selection (Boston: Heath, 1914), to which he usefully added the 'Discourse upon Comedy' also reprinted in *European Theories of the Drama*, edited by Barrett H. Clark (New York: Crown, 1965). There is no separate modern edition of *The Constant Couple*, though it is included in the last of the four volumes of a useful collection, *Restoration Comedy*, edited by A. Norman Jeffares (London: Folio Press, 1974).

George Farquhar has not been a frequent subject for critical monographs. Those available in English are A. J. Farmer's concise, introductory pamphlet in the 'Writers and Their Work' series (London: Longmans, for the British Council, 1966); Eric Rothstein's cogent, detailed study in the 'Twayne's English Authors' series (New York: Twayne, 1967); and Eugene N. James's *The Development of Farquhar as a Comic Dramatist* (The Hague: Mouton, 1972). There is also a straightforward and readable (though occasionally over-conjectural) biography, *Young George Farquhar*, by Willard Connely (London: Cassell, 1949). Few articles in journals deal specifically with *The Constant Couple*, though Richard Morton's 'The Jubilee of 1700 and Farquhar's *The Constant Couple*', in *Notes and Queries*, CC (1955), offers background on the great non-event of the play. Ronald Berman's 'The Comedy of Reason', in *Texas Studies in Literature and Language*, VII (1965), is of related interest.

General studies which deal more than tangentially with Farquhar tend to 'squeeze' him, either chronologically or into their own critical straitjacket. Bonamy Dobrée's *Restoration Comedy 1660-1720* (Oxford: Clarendon Press, 1924) is well-tempered, tolerant, and superficial, while F. S. Boas's *An Introduction to Eighteenth-Century Drama* (Oxford: Clarendon Press, 1953) is little more than doggedly synoptic. Robert D. Hume's *The Development of English Drama in the Late Seventeenth Century* (Oxford: Clarendon Press, 1976) is a far superior work, but although pertinently directed to the problems of our supposedly transitional period, it, too, is relatively neglectful of Farquhar. John Palmer's vintage study *The Comedy of Manners* (London: Bell, 1913) treats our author as a deeply inferior version of Congreve, while H. T. E. Perry's *The Comic Spirit in Restoration Drama* (New York: Russell, 1962) commits the heresy of setting up an arbitrary theory and testing Farquhar (among others) against it. More balanced recent studies include Norman Holland's *The First Modern Comedies* (Harvard University Press, 1959), Kenneth Muir's *The Comedy of Manners* (London, 1970), and Peter Holland's *The Ornament of Action* (Cambridge University Press, 1979).

An otherwise useful collection of essays, *Restoration Drama*, edited by John Loftis (Oxford University Press, 1966) symptomatically includes nothing on Farquhar, though it reprints L. C. Knights's influential attack on the drama of the period, and F. W. Bateson's defence. The standard work on the Collier controversy remains *Comedy and Conscience after the Restoration*, by Joseph Wood Krutch (New York: Columbia University Press, 1924), while John Loftis's *Comedy and Society from Congreve to Fielding* (Stanford University Press, 1959) is helpful on Farquhar as a 'topical' writer.

The fifth volume of *The Revels History of Drama in English* by John Loftis *et al.* (London: Methuen, 1976) covers the period 1660 to 1750, and does deal with the theatre as well as the written drama. But, although the otherwise invaluable theatrical 'calendar', *The London Stage*, cuts Farquhar's career in two (as did Allardyce Nicoll's earlier history), the relevant volumes of the separately-available introduction — *The London Stage 1660-1700: a Critical Introduction*, by Emmett L. Avery and Arthur H. Scouten, and *The London Stage 1700-1729: a Critical Introduction*, by Avery alone (Carbondale: Southern Illinois University Press, 1968) — remain the best general surveys of the theatre of the period. They are 'bridged' by a useful study by Shirley Strum Kenny, 'Theatrical Warfare, 1695-1710', in *Theatre Notebook*, XXVII (1973), which properly highlights the importance of *The Constant Couple* to Drury Lane's success, and some of the essays in *The London Theatre World*, edited by Robert D. Hume (Carbondale: Southern Illinois University Press, 1980), are also helpful. Of the few books on acting and production styles, Jocelyn Powell's stimulating *Restoration Theatre Production* (London: Routledge, 1984) deals at length with Congreve, though scarcely at all with Farquhar, but J. L. Styan's *Restoration Comedy in Performance* (Cambridge University Press, 1986) includes our author in a study especially useful for its investigation of stage conventions.

Director's Note

Farquhar was probably twenty-two when he wrote this play; an Ulsterman who (tradition has it) fought with William of Orange at the Battle of the Boyne, who threw in his studies at Trinity College, Dublin, to become an actor, and in 1697 packed his pen and came to London to make his fortune by writing.

Rising out of the ashes of the Great Fire of thirty years before, London must have made a startling impact on the young writer from Derry. After seventy years of fire, plague, regicide, civil war, rebellion and revolution, the tired old century was limping to an end, and a gleaming new City, greater than any in Europe, was proudly proclaiming its stability, its modernity and its prosperity.

The lessons learned by Farquhar during his time as an actor are well expressed in *The Constant Couple*. He has written wonderful, clearly differentiated roles in a language which is always clear, conversational and precise, and now and then startlingly vernacular and naturalistic. Moreover, unlike the creations of most his contemporaries, and those of his predecessors in the Restoration field, his characters have a capacity for genuine vulnerability. Instead of only satirising and ridiculing the new world to which he was exposed, Farquhar seems to celebrate and applaud it.

The Constant Couple was first played in December 1699, and presumably a performance was given on the eve of the new century itself. The 'Jubilee' celebrated in the subtitle of the play not only commemorates Clincher Senior's abortive attempt to attend the Papal festival in Rome, but also that Great Jubilee being prepared for in London itself, as a bright, confident English metropolitan society, inspired by Peace, Money and Reason, steps optimistically and vigorously into the great new century ahead.

Roger Michell

THE CONSTANT COUPLE
by George Farquhar
(A TRIP TO THE JUBILEE)

THE PROGRAMME

In addition to cast list, biographies and play notes,
the programme you have purchased for this
performance contains the full text of the play.
Please would you bear in mind that following the
text during the performance is very distracting to
the performers especially when you are seated
in rows close to the stage.

Thank you for your help.

Dramatis Personae

MEN

SIR HARRY WILDAIR, *an airy gentleman, affecting humorous gaiety and freedom in his behaviour.*
STANDARD, *disbanded Colonel, brave and generous.*
VIZARD, *outwardly pious, otherwise a great debauchee, and villainous.*
SMUGGLER, *an old merchant.*
CLINCHER SENIOR, *a pert London 'Prentice turned Beau, and affecting travel.*
CLINCHER JUNIOR, *his brother, educated in the Country.*
DICKY, *his man*
TOM ERRAND, *a porter.*

WOMEN

LUREWELL, *a lady of a jilting temper, proceeding from a resentment of her wrongs from men.*
LADY DARLING, *an old lady, mother to Angelica.*
ANGELICA, *a woman of honour.*
PARLY, *maid to Lurewell.*

CONSTABLE, MOB, PORTER'S WIFE, SERVANTS, &c.

The Scene
London.

The Text

The text used and reproduced here is taken from the edition prepared by William Archer for the Mermaid series (New York, Hill & Wang, 1931).

To the Honourable Sir Roger Mostyn, Bart., of Mostyn Hall in Flintshire

SIR, 'Tis no small reflection on pieces of this nature, that panegyric is so much improved, and that dedication is grown more an art than poetry; that authors, to make their patrons more than men, make themselves less; and that persons of honour are forced to decline patronising wit, because their modesty cannot bear the gross strokes of adulation.

But give me leave to say, Sir, that I am too young an author to have learned the art of flattery; and, I hope, the same modesty which recommended this play to the world, will also reconcile my addresses to you, of whom I can say nothing but what your merits may warrant, and all that have the honour of your acquaintance will be proud to vindicate.

The greatest panegyric upon you, Sir, is the unprejudiced and bare truth of your chracter, the fire of youth, with the sedateness of a senator, and the modern gaiety of a fine English gentleman, with the noble solidity of the Ancient Briton.

This is the character, Sir, which all men, but yourself, are proud to publish of you, and which more celebrated pens than mine should transmit to posterity.

The play has had some noble appearances to honour its representation; and to complete the success, I have presumed to prefix so noble a name to usher it into the world. A stately frontispiece is the beauty of a building. But here I must transverse Ovid:

Materia superabit Opus.

I am,

Honourable Sir,

Your most devoted, and

Humble servant,

GEO. FARQUHAR.

PREFACE TO THE READER

An affected modesty is very often the greatest vanity, and authors are sometimes prouder of their blushes than of the praises that occasioned them. I shan't therefore, like a foolish virgin, fly to be pursued, and deny what I chieflly wish for. I am very willing to acknowledge the beauties of this play, especially those of the third night, which not to be proud of were the height of impudence. Who is ashamed to value himself upon such favours, under-values those who conferred them.

As I freely submit to the criticisms of the judicious, so I cannot call this an ill play, since the Town has allowed it such success. When they have pardoned my faults, 'twere very ill manners to condemn their indulgence. Some may think (my acquaintance in town being too slender to make a party for the play) that the success must be derived from the pure merits of the cause. I am of another opinion: I have not been long enough in town to raise enemies against me; and the English are still kind to strangers. I am below the envy of great wits, and above the malice of little ones. I have not displeased the ladies, nor offended the clergy; both which are now pleased to say, that a comedy may be diverting without smut and profaneness.

Next to these advantages, the beauties of action gave the greatest life to the play, of which the town is so sensible, that all will join with me in commendation of the actors, and allow (without detracting from the merits of others) that the Theatre Royal affords an excellent and complete set of comedians. Mr Wilks's performance has set him so far above competition in the part of Wildair, that none can pretend to envy the praise due to his merit. That he made the part, will appear from hence, that whenever the stage has the misfortune to lose him, Sir Harry Wildair may go to the Jubilee.

A great many quarrel at *the Trip to the Jubilee* for a misnomer: I must tell them, that perhaps there are greater trips in the play; and when I find that more exact plays have had better success, I'll talk with the critics about decorums, &c. However, if I ever commit another fault of this nature, I'll endeavour to make it more excusable.

Prologue

BY A FRIEND

Poets will think nothing so checks their fury
As wits, cits, beaux, and women, for their jury
Our spark's half dead to think what medley's come,
With blended judgments to pronounce his doom.
'Tis all false fear; for in a mingled pit,
Why, what your grave don thinks but dully writ,
His neighbour i' th' great wig may take for wit.
Some authors court the few, the wise, if any;
Our youth's content, if he can reach the many,
Who go with much like ends to church and play,
Not to observe what priests or poets say;
No, no, your thoughts, like theirs, lie quite another way.
The ladies safe may smile: for here's no slander,
No smut, no lewd-tongued beau, no *double-entendre*.
'Tis true, he has a spark just come from France,
But then so far from beau – why, he talks sense!
Like coin oft carried out, but – seldom brought from thence.
There's yet a gang to whom our spark submits,
Your elbow-shaking fool, that lives by's wits,
That's only witty though, just as he lives, by fits.
Who, lion-like, through bailiffs scours away,
Hunts, in the face, a dinner all day,
At night, with empty bowels, grumbles o'er the play.
And now the modish prentice he implores,
Who, with his master's cash, stolen out of doors,
Employs it on a brace of – honourable whores;
While their good bulky mother pleased sits by,
Bawd regent of the bubble gallery.
Next to our mounted friends we humbly move,
Who all your side-box tricks are much above,
And never fail to pay us – with your love.
Ah, friends! Poor Dorset-Garden house is gone;
Our merry meetings there are all undone:
Quite lost to us, sure for some strange misdeeds,
That strong dog Samson's pull'd it o'er our heads,
Snaps rope like thread; but when his fortune's told him,
He'll hear perhaps of rope will one day hold him:
At least I hope that our good-natured town
Will find a way to pull his prizes down.
    Well, that's all! Now, gentlemen, for the play.
On second thoughts, I've but two words to say;
Such as it is for your delight design'd,
Hear it, read, try, judge,
and speak as you find.

A New Prologue

*In answer to my very good friend, Mr Oldmixon; who, having two
plays damn'd at the Old House, had a mind to curry favour, to have a
third damn'd at the New.*

'Tis hard the author of this play in view,
Should be condemn'd, purely for pleasing you:
Charged with a crime, which you, his judges, own
Was only this, that he has pleased the town.
He touch'd no poet's verse, nor doctor's bills;
No foe to B —— re, yet a friend to Wills.
No reputation stabb'd by sour debate;
Nor had a hand in bankrupt Brisco's fate:
And, as an ease to's tender conscience, vows,
He's none of those that broke the t'other house:
In perfect pity to their wretched cheer,
Because his play was bad – he brought it here.
The dreadful sin of murder cries aloud;
And sure these poets ne'er can hope for good,
Who dipp'd their barbarous pens in that poor house's blood.
'Twas malice all: no malice like to theirs,
To write good plays, purpose to starve the players.
To starve by's wit, is still the poet's due,
But here are men whose wit's match'd by few;
Their wit both starves themselves and others too.
Our plays are farce, because our house is cramm'd;
Their plays all good; for what? – because they're damn'd.
Because we pleasure you, you call us tools;
And 'cause you please yourselves they call you fools.
By their good-nature, they are wits, true blue;
And men of breeding, by their respects to you.
To engage the fair, all other means being lost,
They fright the boxes with old Shakespeare's ghost;
The ladies of such spectres should take heed;
For 'twas the devil did raise that ghost indeed.
Their case is hard that such despair can show;
They've disobliged all powers above, they know;
And now must have recourse to powers below.
Let Shakespeare then lie still, ghosts do no good;
The fair are better pleased with flesh and blood.
What is't to them, to mind the ancients' taste?
But the poor folks are mad, and I'm in haste.

Runs off.

ACT ONE

Scene One

The Park. Enter Vizard with a letter, Servant following.

VIZARD.

Angelica send it back unopened! say you?

SERVANT.

As you see, sir.

VIZARD.

The pride of these virtuous women is more insufferable than the immodesty of prostitutes! – After all my encouragement, to slight me thus!

SERVANT.

She said, sir, that imagining your morals sincere, she gave you access to her conversation; but that your late behaviour in her company has convinced her that your love and religion are both hypocrisy, and that she believes your letter like yourself, fair on the outside, foul within; so sent it back unopened.

VIZARD.

May obstinacy guard her beauty till wrinkles bury it! Then may desire prevail to make her curse that untimely pride her disappointed age repents! – I'll be revenged the very first opportunity. – Saw you the old Lady Darling, her mother?

SERVANT.

Yes, sir, and she was pleased to say much in your commendation.

VIZARD.

That's my cue. – An esteem grafted in old age is hardly rooted out, years stiffen their opinions with their bodies, and old zeal is only to be cozened by young hypocrisy. – Run to the Lady Lurewell's, and know of her maid whether her ladyship will be at home this evening. – (*Exit Servant.*) Her beauty is sufficient cure for Angelica's scorn. (*Pulls out a book, reads, and walks about.*)

Enter Alderman Smuggler.

SMUGGLER.

Ay, there's a pattern for the young men o' th' times! – At his meditation so early; some book of pious ejaculations, I'm sure.

VIZARD (*aside*).

This Hobbes is an excellent fellow! – (*Aloud.*) O uncle Smuggler! To find you in this end o' th' town is a miracle.

SMUGGLER.

I have seen a miracle this morning indeed, cousin Vizard.

VIZARD.

What is it, pray, sir?

SMUGGLER.

A man at his devotion so near the Court. – I'm very glad, boy, that you keep your sanctity untainted in this infectious place; the very air of this park is heathenish, and every man's breath I meet scents of atheism.

VIZARD.

Surely, sir, some great concern must bring you to this unsanctified end of the town.

SMUGGLER.

A very unsanctified concern truly, cousin.

VIZARD.

What is't?

SMUGGLER.

A lawsuit, boy. – Shall I tell you? – My ship the Swan is newly arrived from St Sebastian's, laden with Portugal wines: now the impudent rogue of a tide-waiter has the face to affirm, 'tis French wines in Spanish casks, and has indicted me upon the statute. – O conscience! conscience! these tide-waiters and surveyors plague us more with their French wines, than the war did with French privateers.

Enter Colonel Standard.

Ay, there's another plague of the nation – a red coat and feather.

VIZARD.

Colonel Standard, I'm your humble servant.

STANDARD.

Maybe not, sir.

VIZARD.

Why so!

STANDARD.

Because – I'm disbanded.

VIZARD.

How? broke!

STANDARD.

This very morning, in Hyde Park, my brave regiment, a thousand men that looked like lions yesterday, were scattered, and looked as poor and simple as the herd of deer that grazed beside 'em.

SMUGGLER (*singing*).

Tal, al, deral! – I'll have a bonfire this night as high as the Monument.

STANDARD.

A bonfire! thou dry, withered, ill nature! had not these brave fellows' swords defended you, your house had been a bonfire ere this about your ears. – Did we not venture our lives, sir?

SMUGGLER.

And did not we pay you for your lives, sir? – Venture your lives! I'm sure we ventured our money, and that's life and soul to me. – Sir, we'll maintain you no longer.

STANDARD.

Then your wives shall, old Actaeon. There are five-and-thirty strapping officers gone this morning to live upon free quarter in the city.

SMUGGLER.

O Lord! O Lord! I shall have a son within these nine months born with a leading staff in his hand. – Sir, you are –

STANDARD.

What, sir?

SMUGGLER.

Sir, I say that you are –

STANDARD.

What, sir?

SMUGGLER.

Disbanded, sir, that's all. – I see my lawyer yonder.

Exit Smuggler.

VIZARD.

Sir, I'm very sorry for your misfortune.

STANDARD.

Why so? I don't come to borrow money of you; if you're my friend, meet me this evening at the Rummer; I'll pay my way, drink a health to my king, prosperity to my country; and away for Hungary tomorrow morning.

VIZARD.

What! you won't leave us?

STANDARD.

What! a soldier stay here! to look like an old pair of colours in Westminster Hall, ragged and rusty! no, no. – I met yesterday a broken lieutenant, he was ashamed to own that he wanted a dinner, but begged eighteenpence of me to buy a new sheath for his sword.

VIZARD.

Oh, but you have good friends, Colonel!

STANDARD.

Oh, very good friends! my father's a lord, and my elder brother a beau.

VIZARD.

But your country may perhaps want your sword again.

STANDARD.

Nay, for that matter, let but a single drum beat up for volunteers between Ludgate and Charing Cross, and I shall undoubtedly hear it at the walls of Buda.

VIZARD.

Come, come, Colonel, there are ways of making your fortune at home. Make your addresses to the fair; you're a man of honour and courage.

STANDARD.

Ay, my courage is like to do me wondrous service with the fair. This pretty cross cut over my eye will attract a duchess. I warrant 'twill be a mighty grace to my ogling. – Had I used the stratagmen of a certain brother colonel of mine, I might succeed.

VIZARD.

What was it, pray?

STANDARD.

Why, to save his pretty face for the women, he always turned his back upon the enemy. He was a man of honour – for the ladies.

VIZARD.

Come, come, the loves of Mars and Venus will never fail; you must get a mistress.

STANDARD.

Prithee, no more on't. You have awakened a thought, from which, and the kingdom, I would have stolen away at once. – To be plain, I have a mistress.

VIZARD.

And she's cruel?

STANDARD.

No.

VIZARD.

Her parents prevent your happiness?

STANDARD.

Nor that.

VIZARD.

Then she has no fortune?

STANDARD.

A large one; beauty to tempt all mankind, and virtue to beat off their assaults. O Vizard! such a creature! – Heyday! who the devil have we here?

VIZARD.

The joy of the playhouse, and life of the Park;

Enter Sir Harry Wildair, crosses the stage singing, with Footmen after him.

Sir Harry Wildair newly come from Paris.

STANDARD.

Sir Harry Wildair! Did not he make a campaign in Flanders some three or four years ago?

VIZARD.

The same.

STANDARD.

Why, he behaved himself very bravely.

VIZARD.

Why not? dost think bravery and gaiety are inconsistent? He's a gentleman of most happy circumstances, born to a plentiful estate, has had a genteel and easy education, free from the rigidness of teachers and pedantry of schools. His florid constitution being never ruffled by misfortune, nor stinted in its pleasures, has rendered him entertaining to others, and easy to himself: – turning all passion into gaiety of humour, by which he chooses rather to rejoice his friends than be hated by any; as you shall see.

Re-enter Wildair, Footman attending.

SIR HARRY.

Ha! Vizard!

VIZARD.

Sir Harry!

SIR HARRY.

Who thought to find you out of the rubric so long? I thought thy hypocrisy had been wedded to a pulpit-cushion long ago. – Sir, if I mistake not your face, your name is Standard.

STANDARD.

Sir Harry, I'm your humble servant.

SIR HARRY.

Come, gentlemen, the news! the news o' th' town! for I'm just arrived.

VIZARD.

Why, in the City end o' th' town we're playing the knave, to get estates.

STANDARD.

And in the Court end, playing the fool in spending 'em.

SIR HARRY.

Just so in Paris; I'm glad we're grown so modish.

VIZARD.

We are all so reformed, that gallantry is taken for vice.

STANDARD.

And hypocrisy for religion.

SIR HARRY.

A la mode de Paris, again.

VIZARD.

Not one whore between Ludgate and Aldgate.

STANDARD.

But ten times more cuckolds than ever.

VIZARD.

Nothing like an oath in the city.

STANDARD.

That's a mistake; for my major swore a hundred and fifty last night to a merchant's wife in her bedchamber.

SIR HARRY.

Psha! this is trifling; tell me news, gentlemen. What lord has lately broke his fortune at the Groom-porter's? or his heart at Newmarket, for the loss of a race? What wife has been lately suing in Doctors' Commons for alimony? or what daughter run away with her father's valet? What beau gave the noblest ball at the Bath, or had the finest coach in the ring? I want news, gentlemen.

STANDARD.

Faith, sir, these are no news at all.

VIZARD.

But pray, Sir Harry, tell us some news of your travels.

SIR HARRY.

With all my heart. You must know, then, I went over to Amsterdam in a Dutch ship; I there had a Dutch whore for five stivers: I went from thence to Landen, where I was heartily drubbed in the battle with the butt-end of a Swiss musket. I thence went to Paris, where I had half a dozen intrigues, bought half a dozen new suits, fought a couple of duels, and here I am again *in statu quo*.

VIZARD.

But we heard that you designed to make the tour of Italy; what brought you back so soon?

SIR HARRY.

That which brought you into the world, and may perhaps carry you out of it: a woman.

STANDARD.

What! quit the pleasures of travel for a woman!

SIR HARRY.

Ay, Colonel, for such a woman! I had rather see her *ruelle* than the palace of Lewis le Grand. There's more glory in her smile than in the Jubilee at Rome; and I would rather kiss her hand than the Pope's toe.

VIZARD.

You, Colonel, have been very lavish in the beauty and virtue of your mistress; and Sir Harry here has been no less eloquent in the praise of his. Now will I lay you both ten guineas a-piece, that neither of them is so pretty, so witty, or so virtuous, as mine.

STANDARD.

'Tis done!

SIR HARRY.

I'll double the stakes. – But, gentlemen, now I think on't, how shall we be resolved? for I know not where my mistress may be found; she left Paris about a month before me, and I had an account –

STANDARD.

How, sir! left Paris about a month before you!

SIR HARRY.

Ay, but I know not where, and perhaps mayn't find her this fortnight.

STANDARD.

Her name! Ay, – she has the softest, whitest hand that ever was made of flesh and blood, her lips so balmy sweet!

STANDARD.

But her name, sir!

SIR HARRY.

Then her neck and breast! – 'Her breasts do so heave, so heave' – (*Singing.*)

VIZARD.

But her name, sir, her quality!

SIR HARRY.

Then her shape, Colonel!

STANDARD.

But her name I want, sir!

SIR HARRY.

Then her eyes, Vizard!

STANDARD.

Psha, Sir Harry, her name or nothing!

SIR HARRY.

Then, if you must have it, she's called the Lady – But then her foot, gentlemen! she dances to a miracle. – Vizard, you have certainly lost your wager.

VIZARD.

Why, you have lost your senses; we shall never discover the picture unless you subscribe the name.

SIR HARRY.

Then her name is Lurewell.

STANDARD (*aside*).

'Sdeath, my mistress!

VIZARD (*aside*).

My mistress, by Jupiter!

SIR HARRY.

Do you know her, gentlemen?

STANDARD.

I have seen her, sir.

SIR HARRY.

Canst tell where she lodges? Tell me, dear colonel.

STANDARD.

Your humble servant, sir.

Exit Colonel Standard.

SIR HARRY.

Nay, hold, Colonel, I'll follow you, and will know.

Runs out.

VIZARD.

The Lady Lurewell his mistress! – He loves her, but she loves me. – But he's a baronet, and I plain Vizard; he has a coach-and-six, and I walk a-foot; I was bred in London, and he in Paris. – That very circumstance has murdered me. – Then, some stratagem must be laid to divert his pretensions.

Re-enter Wildair.

SIR HARRY.

Prithee, Dick, what makes the colonel so out of humour?

VIZARD.

Because he's out of pay, I suppose.

SIR HARRY.

'Slife, that's true! I was beginning to mistrust some rivalship in the case.

VIZARD.

And suppose there were; you know the colonel can fight, Sir Harry.

SIR HARRY.

Fight! psha! but he can't dance, ha! We contend for a woman, Vizard! 'Slife, man, if ladies were to be gained by sword and pistol only, what the devil should all the beaux do?

VIZARD (*aside*).

I'll try him farther. – (*Aloud.*) But would not you, Sir Harry, fight for this woman you so much admire?

SIR HARRY.

Fight? – Let me consider. I love her, that's true; – but then I love honest Sir Harry Wildair better. The Lady Lurewell is divinely charming – right – but, then, a thrust i' th' guts, or a Middlesex jury, is as ugly as the devil.

VIZARD.

Ay, Sir Harry, 'twere a dangerous cast for a beau baronet to be tried by a parcel of greasy, grumbling, bartering boobies, who would hang you purely because you're a gentleman.

SIR HARRY.

Ay, but on the t'other hand, I have money enough to bribe the rogues with: so, upon mature deliberation, I would fight for her. – But no more of her. Prithee, Vizard, can't you recommend a friend to a pretty mistress by the by, till I can find my own? You have store, I'm sure; you cunning poaching dogs make surer game than we that hunt open and fair. Prithee now, good Vizard!

VIZARD.

Let me consider a little. – (*Aside.*) Now love and revenge inspire my politics.

Pauses, whilst Wildair walks singing.

SIR HARRY.

Psha! thou'rt as long studying for a new mistress as a drawer is piercing a new pipe.

VIZARD.

I design a new pipe for you, and wholesome wine; you'll therefore bear a little expectation.

SIR HARRY.

Ha! sayest thou, dear Vizard?

VIZARD.

A girl of sixteen, Sir Harry.

SIR HARRY.

Now sixteen thousand blessings light on thee!

VIZARD.

Pretty and witty.

SIR HARRY.

Ay, ay, but her name, Vizard?

VIZARD.

Her name! yes, – she has the softest, whitest hand that ever was made of flesh and blood, her lips so balmy sweet!

SIR HARRY.

Well, well, but where shall I find her, man?

VIZARD.

Find her! – but, then, her foot, Sir Harry! – she dances to a miracle

SIR HARRY.

Prithee, don't distract me.

VIZARD.

Well, then, you must know that this lady is the curiosit and ambition of the town; her name's Angelica. She that passes for her mother is a private bawd, and called the Lady Darling; she goes for a baronet's lady (no disparagement to your honour, Sir Harry), I assure you.

SIR HARRY.

Psha, hang my honour! But what street, what house?

VIZARD.

Not so fast, Sir Harry; you must have my passport for your admittance, and you'll find my recommendation, in a line or two, will procure you very civil entertainment; I suppose twenty or thirty pieces handsomely placed will gain the point; I'll ensure her sound.

SIR HARRY.

Thou dearest friend to a man in necessity! – (*To Footman.*) Here, sirrah, order my coach about to St James's; I'll walk across the Park.

Exit Footman.

Enter Clincher Senior.

CLINCHER SENIOR.

Here, sirrah, order my coach about to St James's, I'll walk across the Park too. – Mr Vizard, your most devoted. – Sir, (*To* WILDAIR:) I admire the mode of your shoulder-knot; methinks it hangs very emphatically, and carries an air of travel in it; your sword-knot too is most ornamentally modish, and bears a foreign mien. Gentlemen, my brother is just arrived in town, so that, being upon the wing to kiss his hands, I hope you'll pardon this abrupt departure of, gentlemen, your most devoted and most faithful humble servant.

Exit Clincher.

SIR HARRY.

Prithee, dost know him?

VIZARD.

Know him! why 'tis Clincher, who was apprentice to my uncle Smuggler, the merchant in the city.

SIR HARRY.

What makes him so gay?

VIZARD.

Why, he's in mourning for his father; the kind old man, in Hertfordshire t'other day, broke his neck a fox-hunting; the son, upon the news, he broke his indentures, whipped from behind the counter into the side-box, forswears merchandise, where he must live by cheating, and usurps gentility, where he may die by raking. He keeps his coach and liveries, brace of geldings, leash of mistresses, talks of nothing but wines, intrigues, plays, fashions, and going to the Jubilee.

SIR HARRY.

Ha, ha, ha! how many pounds of pulvil must the fellow use in sweetening himself from the smell of hops and tobacco? Faugh! – I' my conscience methought, like Olivia's lover, he stunk of Thames Street. But now for Angelica – that's her name? – We'll to the Princess's chocolate-house, where you shall write my passport. *Allons.*

Exeunt

Scene Two

Lady Lurewell's Lodgings. Lady Lurewell and her Maid Parly.

LADY LUREWELL.

Parly, my pocket-book! – Let me see – Madrid, Venice, Paris, London. – Ay, London! They may talk what they will of the hot countries, but I find love most fruitful under this climate. – In a month's space I have gained – let me see – *imprimis,* Colonel Standard.

PARLY.

And how will your ladyship manage him?

LADY LUREWELL.

As all soldiers should be managed: he shall serve me till I gain my ends, then I disband him.

PARLY.

But he loves you, madam.

LADY LUREWELL.

Therefore I scorn him. I hate all that don't love me, and slight all that do. Would his whole deluding sex admire me, thus would I slight them all! My virgin and unwary innocence was wronged by faithless man, but now glances eyes, plot brain, dissemble face, lie tongue, and be a second Eve to tempt, seduce and damn the treacherous kind. Let me survey my captives. – The Colonel leads the van; next Mr Vizard, he courts me, out of the *Practice of Piety,* therefore is a hypocrite; then Clincher, he adores me with orangery, and is consequently a fool; then my old merchant Alderman Smuggler, he's a compound of both; out of which medley of lovers, if I don't make good diversion – what d'ye think, Parly?

PARLY.

I think, madam, I'm like to be very virtuous in your service, if you teach me all those tricks that you use to your lovers.

LADY LUREWELL.

You're a fool, child; observe this, that though a woman swear, forswear, lie, dissemble, back-bite, be proud, vain, malicious, anything, if she secures the main chance, she's still virtuous; that's a maxim.

PARLY.

I can't be persuaded though, madam, but that you really loved Sir Harry Wildair in Paris.

LADY LUREWELL.

Of all the lovers I ever had, he was my greatest plague, for I could never make him uneasy; I left him involved in a duel upon my account; I long to know whether the fop be killed or not.

Enter Standard.

Lord! no sooner talk of killing, but the soldier is conjured up. You're upon hard duty, Colonel, to serve your king, your country, and a mistress too.

STANDARD.

The latter, I must confess, is the hardest; for in war, madam, we can be relieved in our duty: but in love who would take our post is our enemy; emulation in glory is transporting, but rivals here intolerable.

LADY LUREWELL.

Those that bear away the prize in the field, should boast the same success in the bedchamber; and I think, considering the weakness of our sex, we should make those our companions who can be our champions.

STANDARD.

I once, madam, hoped the honour of defending you from all injuries through a title to your lovely person; but now my love must attend my fortune. This commission, madam, was my passport to the fair; adding a nobleness to my passion, it stamped a value on my love; 'twas once the life of honour, but now its hearse, and with it must my love be buried.

PARLY.

What! disbanded, colonel?

STANDARD.

Yes, Mrs Parly.

PARLY (*aside*).

Faugh, the nauseous fellow! he stinks of poverty already.

LADY LUREWELL (*aside*).

His misfortune troubles me, 'cause it may prevent my designs.

STANDARD.

I'll choose, madam, rather to destroy my passion by absence abroad, than have it starved at home.

LADY LUREWELL.

I'm sorry, sir, you have so mean an opinion of my affection, as to imagine it founded upon your fortune. And to convince you of your mistake, here I vow by all that's sacred, I own the same affection now as before. Let it suffice, my fortune is considerable.

STANDARD.

No, madam, no; I'll never be a charge to her I love. The man that sells himself for gold is the worst of prostitutes.

LADY LUREWELL (*aside*).

Now were he any other creature but a man, I could love him.

STANDARD.

This only last request I make, that not title recommend a fool, office introduce a knave, nor a coat a coward, to my place in your affections; so farewell my country! and adieu my love!

Exit Colonel Standard.

LADY LUREWELL.

Now the devil take thee for being so honourable! – Here, Parly, call him back. – (*Exit Parly.*) I shall lose half my diversion else.

Re-enter Parly with Standard.

Now for a trial of skill. – Sir, I hope you'll pardon my curiosity; when do you take your journey?

STANDARD.

Tomorrow morning, early, madam

LADY LUREWELL.

So suddenly! Which way are you designed to travel?

STANDARD.

That I can't yet resolve on.

LADY LUREWELL.

Pray sir, tell me, pray sir, I entreat you. Why are you so obstinate?

STANDARD.

Why are you so curious, madam?

LADY LUREWELL.

Because –

STANDARD.

What?

LADY LUREWELL.

Because, I – I –

STANDARD.

Because what, madam? Pray tell me.

LADY LUREWELL.

Because I design – to follow you. (*Crying.*)

STANDARD.

Follow me! by all that's great! I ne'er was proud before, but love from such a creature might swell the vanity of the proudest prince. Follow me! By Heavens, thou shalt not.

What! expose thee to the hazards of a camp! – Rather I'll stay and here bear the contempt of fools, and worst of fortune.

LADY LUREWELL.
You need not, shall not; my estate for both is sufficient.

STANDARD.
Thy estate! no, I'll turn a knave and purchase one myself; I'll cringe to that proud man I undermine, and fawn on him that I would bite to death; I'll tip my tongue with flattery, and smooth my face with smiles; I'll turn pimp, informer, office-broker, nay coward, to be great; and sacrifice it all to thee, my generous fair.

LADY LUREWELL.
And I'll dissemble, lie, swear, jilt, anything but I'll reward thy love, and recompense thy noble passion.

STANDARD.
Sir Harry, ha, ha, ha! poor Sir Harry, ha, ha, ha! Rather kiss her hand than the Pope's toe, ha ha, ha!

LADY LUREWELL.
What Sir Harry? Colonel, what Sir Harry?

STANDARD.
Sir Harry Wildair, madam –

LADY LUREWELL.
What! is he come over?

STANDARD.
Ay, and he told me – but I don't beieve a syllable on't.

LADY LUREWELL.
What did he tell you?

STANDARD.
Only called you his mistress, and pretending to be extravagant in your commendation, would vainly insinuate the praise of his own judgment and good fortune in a choice –

LADY LUREWELL.
How easily is the vanity of fops tickled by our sex!

STANDARD.
Why, your sex is the vanity of fops.

LADY LUREWELL.
O; my conscience, I believe so. This gentleman, because he danced well, I pitched on for a partner at a ball in Paris, and ever since he has so persecuted me with letters, songs, dances, serenading, flattery, foppery and noise, that I was forced to fly the kingdom. – And I warrant you he made you jealous?

STANDARD.
Faith, madam, I was a little uneasy.

LADY LUREWELL.
You shall have a plentiful revenge. I'll send him back all his foolish letters, songs, and verses, and you yourself shall carry 'em; 'twill afford you opportunity of triumphing, and free me from his farther impertinence; for of all men he's my aversion. – I'll run and fetch them instantly.

STANDARD.
Dear madam, a rare project! – (Exit Lady Lurewell.) How I shall bait him like Actaeon, with his own dogs! – Well, Mrs Parly, 'tis ordered by Act of Parliament, that you receive no more pieces, Mrs Parly. –

PARLY
'Tis provided by the same act, that you send no more messages by me, good Colonel; you must not pretend to send any more letters, unless you can pay the postage.

STANDARD.
Come, come, don't be mercenary; take example by your lady, be honourable.

PARLY.
A lack a day, sir! it shows as ridiculous and haughty for us to imitate our betters in their honour as in their finery; leave honour to nobility that can support it; we poor folks, Colonel, have no pretence to't; and truly, I think, sir that your honour should be cashiered with your leading-staff.

STANDARD (aside).
'Tis one of the greatest curses of poverty to be the jest of chambermaids!

Re-enter Lady Lurwell.

LADY LUREWELL.
Here's the packet, Colonel; the whole magazine of love's artillery. (Gives him the packet.)

STANDARD.
Which since I have gained I will turn upon the enemy. Madam, I'll bring you the news of my victory this evening. – Poor Sir Harry, ha, ha, ha!

Exit Colonel Standard.

LADY LUREWELL.
To the right about! as you were! – march, Colonel! ha, ha, ha!
Vain man, who boasts of studied parts and wiles,
Nature in us your deepest art beguiles,
Stamping deep cunning in our frowns and smiles.
You toil for art, your intellects you trace;
Woman, without a thought, bears policy in her face.

ACT TWO

Scene One

Clincher Junior's Lodgings. Enter Clincher Junior, opening a letter, Dicky following.

CLINCHER JUNIOR (*reads*).
Dear Brother,
I will see you presently. I have sent this lad to wait on you; he can instruct you in the fashions of the town. I am your affectionate brother,
Clincher
Very well, and what's your name, sir?

DICKY.
My name is Dicky, sir.

CLINCHER JUNIOR.
Dicky!

DICKY.
Ay, Dicky, sir.

CLINCHER JUNIOR.
Very well, a pretty name! And what can you do, Mr Dicky?

DICKY.
Why, sir, I can powder a wig, and pick up a whore.

CLINCHER JUNIOR.
O Lord! O Lord! – a whore! Why, are there many whores in this town?

DICKY.
Ha, ha, ha! many whores? there's a question indeed! Why, sir, there are above five hundred surgeons in town. Hark'ee, sir, do you see that woman there in the velvet scarf, and red knots?

CLINCHER JUNIOR.
Ay, sir; what then?

DICKY.
Why. she shall be at your service in three minutes, as I'm a pimp.

CLINCHER JUNIOR.
O Jupiter Ammon! why, she's a gentlewoman.

DICKY.
A gentlewoman! why so are all the whores in town, sir.

Enter Clincher Senior.

CLINCHER SENIOR.
Brother, you're welcome to London.

CLINCHER JUNIOR.
I thought, brother, you owed so much to the memory of my father as to wear mourning for his death.

CLINCHER SENIOR.
Why, so I do, fool: I wear this because I have the estate, and you wear that because you have not the estate: you have cause to mourn indeed, brother. Well, brother I'm glad to see you, fare you well!
Going.

CLINCHER JUNIOR.
Stay, stay, brother! Where are you going?

CLINCHER SENIOR.
How natural 'tis for a country booby to ask impertinent questions! – Hark'ee, sir, is not my father dead?

CLINCHER JUNIOR.
Ay, ay, to my sorrow.

CLINCHER SENIOR.
No matter for that, he's dead. And am not I a young powdered extravagant English sir?

CLINCHER JUNIOR.
Very right, sir.

CLINCHER SENIOR.
Why, then, sir, you may be sure that I am going to the Jubilee, sir.

CLINCHER JUNIOR.
Jubilee! what's that?

CLINCHER SENIOR.
Jubilee! why, the Jubilee is – faith, I don't know what it is.

DICKY.
Why, the Jubilee is the same thing with our Lord Mayor's day in the city; there will be pageants, and squibs, and raree-shows, and all that, sir.

CLINCHER JUNIOR.
And must you go so soon, brother?

CLINCHER SENIOR.
Yes, sir, for I must stay a month in Amsterdam, to study poetry.

CLINCHER JUNIOR.
Then I suppose, brother, you travel through Muscovy to learn fashions, don't you brother?

CLINCHER SENIOR.
Brother! – Prithee, Robin, don't call me brother; 'Sir' will do every jot as well.

CLINCHER JUNIOR.
O Jupiter Ammon! why so?

CLINCHER SENIOR.
Because people will imagine that you have a spite at me, – But have you seen your cousin Angelica yet, and her mother the Lady Darling?

CLINCHER JUNIOR.
No, my dancing-master has not been with me yet. How shall I salute them, brother?

CLINCHER SENIOR.
Psha! that's easy; 'tis only two scrapes, a kiss, and your humble servant; I'll tell you more when I come from the Jubilee. Come along.

Exeunt

Scene Two

Lady Darling's house. Enter Wildair, with a letter.

SIR HARRY.
Like light and heat incorporate we lay,
We bless'd the night, and cursed the coming day.

Well, if this paper-kite flies sure, I'm secure of my game. – Humph! the prettiest bordel I have seen; a very stately genteel one –

Footmen cross the stage.

Hey-day! equipage too! Now for a bawd by the courtesy, and a whore with a coat of arms. – 'Sdeath, I'm afraid I've mistaken the house!

Enter Lady Darling.

No, this must be the bawd by her bulk,

LADY DARLING.
Your business, pray, sir?

SIR HARRY.
Pleasure, madam.

LADY DARLING.
Then, sir, you have no business here.

SIR HARRY.
This letter, madam, will inform you farther; Mr Vizard sent it, with his humble service to your ladyship.

LADY DARLING.
How does my cousin, sir?

SIR HARRY (*aside*).
Ay, her cousin too: – that's right procuress again.

LADY DARLING (*reads*).
Madam – earnest inclination to serve – Sir Harry – madam – court my cousin – gentleman – fortune – your ladyship's most humble servant, – Vizard.
Sir, your fortune and quality are sufficient to recommend you anywhere; but what goes farther with me is the recommendation of so sober and pious a young gentleman as my cousin Vizard.

SIR HARRY (*aside*).
A right sanctified bawd, o' my world!

LADY DARLING.
Sir Harry, your conversation with Mr Vizard argues you a gentleman, free from the loose and vicious carriage of the town; I'll therefore call my daughter.

Exit.

SIR HARRY.
Now go thy way for an illustrious bawd of Babylon! – She dresses up a sin so religiously, that the devil would hardly know it of his making.

Re-enter Lady Darling with Angelica.

LADY DARLING (*aside to Angelica*).
Pray, daughter, use him civilly; such matches won't offer every day.

Exit.

SIR HARRY (*aside*).
O all ye powers of love! an angel! 'Sdeath, what money have I got in my pocket? I can't offer her less than twenty guineas – and, by Jupiter, she's worth a hundred!

ANGELICA (*aside*).
'Tis he! the very same? and his person as agreeable as his character of good-humour. – Pray Heaven his silence proceed from respect.

SIR HARRY (*aside*).

How innocent she looks! How would that modesty adorn virtue, when it makes even vice look so charming! By Heaven, there's such a commanding innocence in her looks that I dare not ask the question.

ANGELICA (*aside*).

Now all the charms of real love and feigned indifference assist me to engage his heart, for mine is lost already.

SIR HARRY.

Madam – I, I – (*Aside.*) Zoons! I cannot speak to her. – But she's a whore, and I will. – (*Aloud.*) Madam, in short, I, I – (*Aside.*) O hypocrisy, hypocrisy! what a charming sin art thou!

ANGELICA (*aside*).

He is caught; now to secure my conquest. – (*Aloud.*) I thought, sir, you had business to impart?

SIR HARRY (*aside*).

Business to impart! how nicely she words it! – (*Aloud.*) Yes, madam; don't you – don't you love singing birds, madam?

ANGELICA (*aside*).

That's an odd question for a lover. – (*Aloud.*) Yes, sir.

SIR HARRY.

Why, then, madam, here is a nest of the prettiest goldfinches that ever chirped in a cage; twenty young ones, I assure you madam.

ANGELICA.

Twenty young ones! what then, sir?

SIR HARRY.

Why, then, madam, there are twenty young ones. – 'Slife, I think twenty is pretty fair.

ANGELICA (*aside*).

He's mad, sure! – (*Aloud.*) Sir Harry, when you have learned more wit and manners you shall be welcome here again.

Exit.

SIR HARRY.

Wit and manners! Egad, now I conceive there is a great deal of wit and manners in twenty guineas. – I'm sure 'tis all the wit and manners I have about me at present. What shall I do?

Enter Clincher Junior and Dicky.

What the devil's here? Another cousin, I warrant ye! –

Hark'ee, sir, can you lend me ten or a dozen guineas instantly? I'll pay you fifteen for them in three hours, upon my honour.

CLINCHER JUNIOR (*aside to Dicky*).

These London sparks are plaguy impudent! This fellow, by his wig and assurance, can be no less than a courtier.

DICKY.

He's rather a courtier by his borrowing.

CLINCHER JUNIOR.

Faith, sir, I han't above five guineas about me.

SIR HARRY.

What business have you here then, sir? For to my knowledge twenty won't be sufficient.

CLINCHER JUNIOR.

Sufficient! for what, sir?

SIR HARRY.

What, sir! why, for that, sir; what the devil should it be, sir! I know your business notwithstanding all your gravity sir.

CLINCHER JUNIOR.

My business! why, my cousin lives here.

SIR HARRY.

I know your cousin does live here and Vizard's cousin, and – my cousin, and everybody's cousin. – Hark'ee, sir, I shall return immediately, and if you offer to touch her till I come back, I shall cut your throat, rascal!

Exit.

CLINCHER JUNIOR.

Why, the man's mad, sure!

DICKY.

Mad, sir! ay. Why, he's a beau!

CLINCHER JUNIOR.

A beau! what's that? Are all madmen beaux?

DICKY.

No, sir; but most beaux are madmen. – But now for your cousin. Remember your three scrapes, a kiss, and your humble servant.

Exeunt, as into the house.

Scene Three

The Street. Enter Wildair, Standard following.

STANDARD.
Sir Harry! Sir Harry!

SIR HARRY.
I'm in haste, Colonel; besides, if you're in no better humour than when I parted with you in the Park this morning, your company won't be very agreeable.

STANDARD.
You're a happy man, Sir Harry, who are never out of humour. Can nothing move your gall, Sir Harry?

SIR HARRY.
Nothing but impossibilities, which are the same as nothing.

STANDARD.
What impossibilities?

SIR HARRY.
The resurrection of my father to disinherit me, or an Act of Parliament against wenching. A man of eight thousand pounds per annum to be vexed! – No, no; anger and spleen are companions for younger brothers.

STANDARD.
Suppose one called you son of a whore behind your back?

SIR HARRY.
Why, then would I call him rascal behind his back, and so we're even.

STANDARD.
But suppose you had lost a mistress?

SIR HARRY.
Why, then would I get another.

STANDARD.
But suppose you were discarded by the woman you love, that would surely trouble you?

SIR HARRY.
You're mistaken, Colonel; my love is neither romantically honourable, nor meanly mercenary. 'Tis only a pitch of gratitude: while she loves me, I love her; when she desists, the obligation's void.

STANDARD.
But to be mistaken in your opinion, sir; if the Lady Lurewell (only suppose it) had discarded you – I say, only suppose it – and had sent your discharge by me!

SIR HARRY.
Psha! that's another impossibility.

STANDARD.
Are you sure of that?

SIR HARRY.
Why, 'twere a solecism in nature! – we're finger and thumb, sir. She dances with me, sings with me, plays with me, lies with me!

STANDARD.
How, sir?

SIR HARRY.
I mean in an honourable way; that is, she lies for me. – In short, we are as like one another as a couple of guineas!

STANDARD.
Now that I have raised you to the highest pinnacle of vanity, will I give you so mortifying a fall as shall dash your hopes to pieces! – I pray your honour to peruse these papers.

Gives him the packet.

SIR HARRY.
What is't? The muster-roll of your regiment, Colonel?

STANDARD.
No, no, 'tis a list of your forces in your last love campaign; and for your comfort, all disbanded!

SIR HARRY.
Prithee, good metaphorical Colonel, what d'ye mean?

STANDARD.
Read, sir, read! these are the Sibyl's leaves that will unfold your destiny.

SIR HARRY.
So it be not a false deed to cheat me of my estate, what care I! – (*Opening the packet.*) Humph! my hand! –To the Lady Lurewell! – To the Lady Lurewell! – To the Lady Lurewell! – What devil hast thou been tampering with to conjure up these spirits?

STANDARD.
A certain familiar of your acquaintance, sir.

SIR HARRY (*reading*).
Madam, my passion – so natural – your beauty contending – force of charms – mankind – eternal admirer, Wildair! –
I was never ashamed of my name before!

STANDARD.

What, Sir Harry Wildair out of humour! ha, ha, ha! – Poor Sir Harry! more glory in her smile than in the Jubilee at Rome, ha, ha, ha! – But then her foot, Sir Harry! she dances to a miracle, ha, ha ha! – Fy, Sir Harry! a man of your parts write letters not worth a keeping! – What say'st thou, my dear knight-errant? ha, ha, ha! – You may go seek adventures now indeed!

SIR HARRY (*sings*).

No no, let her wander,' &c.

STANDARD.

You are jilted to some tune, sir! blown up with false music, that's all!

SIR HARRY.

Now, why should I be angry that a woman is a woman? Since inconstancy and falsehood are grounded in their natures, how can they help it?

STANDARD.

Then they must be grounded in your nature; for you and she are finger and thumb, sir!

SIR HARRY.

Here's a copy of verses, too; I must turn poet in the devil's name! – (*Aside*.) Stay! – 'sdeath, what's here? This is her hand. – Oh, the charming characters! – (*Reading*.) My dear Wildair, – That's I; – this huff bluff colonel – that's he, – is the rarest fool in nature, – the devil he is! – and as such have I used him; – with all my heart, faith! – I had no better way of letting you know that I lodge in Pall Mall, near the Holy Lamb. – (*Aloud*.) Colonel, I'm your most humble servant.

STANDARD.

Hold sir! you shan't go yet; I han't delivered half my message.

SIR HARRY.

Upon my faith, but you have, Colonel!

STANDARD.

Well, well, own your spleen; out with it: I know you're like to burst.

SIR HARRY.

I am so, by Gad, ha, ha, ha!

STANDARD.

Ay, with all my heart, ha, ha! – (*Laugh and point at one another*.) Well, well that's all forced, Sir Harry.

SIR HARRY.

I was never better pleased in all my life, by Jupiter

STANDARD.

Well, Sir Harry, 'tis prudence to hide your concern when there's no help for't. – But to be serious now, the lady has sent you back all your papers there. I was so just as not to look upon 'em.

SIR HARRY.

I'm glad on't, sir; for there were some things that I would not have you see.

STANDARD.

All this she has done for my sake, and I desire you would decline any farther pretensions for your own sake. So, honest, good-natured Sir Harry, I'm your humble servant.

Exit.

SIR HARRY.

Ha, ha, ha! poor Colonel! – Oh, the delight, of an ingenious mistress! what a life and briskness it adds to an amour! like the loves of mighty Jove, still suing in different shapes. A legerdemain mistress, who, *Presto! pass!* and she's vanished, then *Hey!* in an instant in your arms again.

Going.

Enter Vizard.

VIZARD.

Well met, Sir Harry; what news from the island of Love?

SIR HARRY.

Faith, we made but a broken voyage by your card; but now I am bound for another port: I told you the colonel was my rival.

VIZARD (*aside*).

The colonel! cursed misfortune! another!

SIR HARRY.

But the civillest in the world: he brought me word where my mistress lodges. The story's too long to tell you now, for I must fly.

VIZARD.

What! have you given over all thoughts of Angelica?

SIR HARRY.

No, no, I'll think of her some other time. But now for the Lady Lurewell; wit and beauty calls.
That mistress ne'er can pall her lover's joys,
Whose wit can whet whene'er her beauty cloys.

Her little amorous frauds all truths excel,
And make us happy, being deceived so well.

Exit.

VIZARD.

The colonel, my rival too! how shall I manage? There is but one way: him and the knight will I set a-tilting, where one cuts t'other's throat, and the survivor's hanged. So there will be two rivals pretty decently disposed of. Since honour may oblige them to play the fool, why should not necessity engage me to play the knave?

Exit.

Scene Four

Lady Lurewell's Lodgings. Lurewell and Parly.

LADY LUREWELL.

Has my servant brought me the money from my merchant?

PARLY.

No, madam, he met Alderman Smuggler at Charing Cross, who has promised to wait on you himself immediately.

LADY LUREWELL.

'Tis odd that this old rogue should pretend to love me, and at the same time cheat me of my money.

PARLY.

'Tis well, madam, if he don't cheat you of your estate; for you say the writings are in his hands.

LADY LUREWELL.

But what satisfaction can I get of him? –

Enter Alderman Smuggler.

Mr Alderman, your servant. Have you brought me any money, sir?

SMUGGLER.

Faith, madam, trading is very dead; what with paying the taxes, raising the customs, losses at sea abroad, and maintaining our wives at home, the bank is reduced very low.

LADY LUREWELL.

Come, come, sir, these evasions won't serve your turn; I must have money, sir; – I hope you don't design to cheat me.

SMUGGLER.

Cheat you, madam! have a care what you say: I'm an alderman, madam. Cheat you, madam! I have been an honest citizen these five-and-thirty years!

LADY LUREWELL.

An honest citizen! bear witness, Parly! I shall trap him in more lies presently. – Come, sir, though I'm a woman I can take a course.

SMUGGLER.

What course, madam? You'll go to law, will ye? I can maintain a suit of law, be it right or wrong, these forty years. I'm sure of that, thanks to the honest practice of the court.

LADY LUREWELL.

Sir, I'll blast your reputation, and so ruin your credit.

SMUGGLER.

Blast my reputation! he, he, he! – Why, I'm a religious man, madam! I have been very instrumental in the reformation of manners. Ruin my credit! ah, poor woman. There is but one way, madam, – you have a sweet leering eye!

LADY LUREWELL.

You instrumental in reformation! How?

SMUGGLER.

I whipped all the whores, cut and long tail, out of the parish. – Ah! that leering eye! – Then I voted for pulling down the playhouse. – Ah, that ogle! that ogle! – Then my own pious example. – Ah, that lip! that lip!

LADY LUREWELL (*aside to Parly*).

Here's a religious rogue for you now! As I hope to be saved, I have a good mind to beat the old monster.

SMUGGLER.

Madam, I have brought you about a hundred and fifty guineas (a great deal of money as times go), and –

LADY LUREWELL.

Come, give it me.

SMUGGLER.

Ah, that hand! that hand! that pretty, soft, white – I have brought it, you see; but the condition of the obligation is such, that whereas that leering eye, that pouting lip, that pretty soft hand, that – you understand me; you understand, I'm sure you do, you little rogue –

LADY LUREWELL (*aside to Parly*).

Here's a villain now, so covetous, that he won't wench upon his own cost, but would bribe me with my own money! I will be revenged. – (*Aloud.*) Upon my word, Mr Alderman, you make me blush; what d'ye mean, pray?

SMUGGLER.

See here, madam. – (*Puts a piece of money in his mouth.*) Buss and guinea, buss and guinea, buss and guinea!

LADY LUREWELL.
Well, Mr Alderman, you have such pretty yellow teeth and green gums, that I will – ha, ha ha, ha!

SMUGGLER.
Will you indeed? he, he, he! my little cocket; and when? and where? and how?

LADY LUREWELL.
'Twill be a difficult point, sir, to secure both our honours: you must therefore be disguised, Mr Alderman.

SMUGGLER.
Psha! no matter, I am an old fornicator, I'm not half so religious as I seem to be. You little rogue; why, I am disguised as I am; our sanctity is all outside, all hypocrisy.

LADY LUREWELL.
No man is seen to come into this house after nightfall; you must therefore sneak in when 'tis dark, in woman's clothes.

SMUGGLER.
Egad so! cod so! – I have a suit a purpose, my little cocket! I love to be disguised; ecod, I make a very handsome woman, ecod, I do!

Enter Footman, whispers Lady Lurewell and exit.

LADY LUREWELL.
Oh! Mr Alderman, shall I beg you to walk into the next room? here are some strangers coming up.

SMUGGLER.
Buss and guinea first; ah, my little cocket!

Exit.

Enter Wildair, Footman attending.

SIR HARRY.
My life, my soul, my all that heaven can give!

LADY LUREWELL.
Death's life with thee, without thee death to live.
Welcome, my dear Sir Harry, I see you got my directions.

SIR HARRY.
Directions! in the most charming manner, thou dear Machiavel of intrigue!

LADY LUREWELL.
Still brisk and airy, I find, Sir Harry.

SIR HARRY.
The sight of you, madam, exalts my air, and makes joy lighten in my face

LADY LUREWELL.
I have a thousand questions to ask you, Sir Harry. How d'ye like France?

SIR HARRY.
Ah! est le plus beau pays du monde.

LADY LUREWELL.
Then what made you leave it so soon?

SIR HARRY.
Madame vous voyez que je vous suis partout.

LADY LUREWELL.
O monsieur, je vous suis fort obligée. – But where's the Court now?

SIR HARRY.
At Marli, madam.

LADY LUREWELL.
And where my Count Le Valier?

SIR HARRY.
His body's in the church of Nôtre Dame; I don't know where his soul is.

LADY LUREWELL.
What disease did he die of?

SIR HARRY.
A duel, madam; I was his doctor.

LADY LUREWELL.
How d'ye mean?

SIR HARRY.
As most doctors do, I killed him!

LADY LUREWELL.
En cavalier, my dear knight-errant? Well, and how? And how? What intrigues, what gallantries are carrying on in the *beau-monde?*

SIR HARRY.
I should ask you that question, madam, since your ladyship makes the *beau-monde* wherever you come.

LADY LUREWELL.
Ah, Sir Harry! I've been almost ruined, pestered to death here, by the incessant attacks of a mighty colonel; he has besieged me as close as our army did Namur.

SIR HARRY.
I hope your ladyship did not surrender though?

LADY LUREWELL.
No, no, but was forced to capitulate; but since you are come to raise the siege, we'll dance, and sing, and laugh.

SIR HARRY.
And love and kiss. – *Montrez-moi vôtre chambre.*

LADY LUREWELL.
Attende, attende, un peu. – I remember, Sir Harry, you promised me in Paris never to ask that impertinent question again.

SIR HARRY.
Psha, madam! that was above two months ago; besides, madam, treaties made in France are never kept.

LADY LUREWELL.
Would you marry me, Sir Harry?

SIR HARRY.
Oh! – *Le mariage est un grand mal* – but I will marry you.

LADY LUREWELL.
Your word, sir, is not to be relied on: if a gentleman will forfeit his honour in dealings of business, we may reasonably suspect his fidelity in an amour.

SIR HARRY.
My honour in dealings of business! Why, madam, I never had any business in all my life.

LADY LUREWELL.
Yes, Sir Harry, I have heard a very odd story, and am sorry that a gentleman of your figure should undergo the scandal.

SIR HARRY.
Out with it, madam.

LADY LUREWELL.
Why, the merchant, sir, that transmitted your bills of exchange to you in France, complains of some indirect and dishonourable dealings.

SIR HARRY.
Who, old Smuggler!

LADY LUREWELL.
Ay, ay, you know him, I find.

SIR HARRY.
I have no less than reason, I think; why, the rogue has cheated me of about five hundred pound within these three years.

LADY LUREWELL.
'Tis your business then to acquit yourself publicly; for he spreads the scandal everywhere.

SIR HARRY.
Acquit myself publicly! – (*To Footman:*) Here, sirrah, my coach; I'll drive instantly into the City, and cane the old villain round the Royal Exchange; he shall run the gauntlet through a thousand brushed beavers and formal cravats.

LADY LUREWELL.
Why, he is in the house now, sir.

SIR HARRY.
What, in this house?

LADY LUREWELL.
Ay, in the next room.

SIR HARRY.
Then, sirrah, lend me your cudgel.

LADY LUREWELL.
Sir Harry, you won't raise a disturbance in my house.

SIR HARRY.
Disturbance, madam! no, no, I'll beat him with the temper of a philosopher. – Here, Mrs Parly, show me the gentleman.

Exit with Parly and Footman.

LADY LUREWELL.
Now shall I get the old monster well beaten, and Sir Harry pestered next term with bloodsheds, batteries, costs and damages, solicitors and attorneys; and if they don't tease him out of his good humour, I'll never plot again.

Exit.

Scene Five

Changes to another room in the same house. Alderman Smuggler discovered alone.

SMUGGLER.
Oh, this damned tide-waiter! A ship and cargo worth five thousand pound! why, 'tis richly worth five hundred perjuries.

Enter Wildair.

SIR HARRY.
Dear Mr Alderman, I'm your most devoted and humble servant.

SMUGGLER.
My best friend, Sir Harry! You're welcome to England.

SIR HARRY.

I'll assure you, sir, there's not a man in the king's dominions I'm gladder to meet.

SMUGGLER.

O Lord, sir, you travellers have the most obliging ways with you!

SIR HARRY.

There is a business, Mr Alderman, fallen out, which you may oblige me infinitely by – I am very sorry that I am forced to be troublesome; but necessity. Mr Alderman –

SMUGGLER.

Ay, sir, as you say, necessity – but upon my word, sir, I am very short of money, at present, but –

SIR HARRY.

That's not the matter, sir, I'm above an obligation that way; but the business is, I am reduced to an indispensable necessity of being obliged to you for a beating. Here, take this cudgel.

SMUGGLER.

A beating, Sir Harry! ha, ha, ha! I beat a knight-baronet! an alderman turn cudgel-player! ha, ha, ha!

SIR HARRY.

Upon my word, sir, you must beat me, or I cudgel you; take your choice.

SMUGGLER.

Psha, psha, you jest!

SIR HARRY.

Nay, 'tis as sure as fate: so, Alderman, I hope you'll pardon my curiosity.

Strikes him.

SMUGGLER.

Curiosity! deuce take your curiosity, sir! what d'ye mean?

SIR HARRY.

Nothing at all: I'm but in jest, sir.

SMUGGLER.

Oh, I can take anything in jest; but a man might imagine by the smartness of the stroke that you were in downright earnest.

SIR HARRY.

Not in the least, sir; – (*Strikes him.*) not in the least, indeed, sir!

SMUGGLER.

Pray, good sir, no more of your jests: for they are the bluntest jests that I ever knew

SIR HARRY (*strikes*).

I heartily beg your pardon, with all my heart, sir.

SMUGGLER.

Pardon, sir! well sir, that is satisfaction enough from a gentleman; but seriously now, if you pass any more of your jests upon me, I shall grow angry.

SIR HARRY.

I humbly beg your permission to break one or two more.

Striking him.

SMUGGLER.

O Lord, sir, you'll break my bones! Are you mad, sir? Murder! felony! manslaughter!

Wildair knocks him down.

SIR HARRY.

Sir, I beg you ten thousand pardons! but I am absolutely compelled to't, upon my honour, sir; nothing can be more averse to my inclinations than to jest with my honest, dear, loving, obliging friend, the alderman.

Striking him all this while. Smuggler tumbles over and over, and shakes out his pocket-book on the floor.

Enter Lady Lurewell.

LADY LUREWELL (*aside*).

The old rogue's pocket-book; this may be of use – (*Takes it up.*) O Lord, Sir Harry's murdering the poor old man!

SMUGGLER.

O dear, madam, I was beaten in jest, till I am murdered in good earnest.

LADY LUREWELL.

Well, well, I'll bring you off. – (*To Sir Harry:*) *Seigneur, frappez, frappez!*

SMUGGLER.

Oh, for charity's sake, madam, rescue a poor citizen!

LADY LUREWELL.

Oh you barbarous man! hold, hold! – *Frappez plus rudement, frappez!* – I wonder you are not ashamed! – (*Holding Sir Harry.*) A poor reverend honest elder! – (*Helps Smuggler up.*) It makes me weep to see him in this condition, poor man! – Now the devil take you, Sir Harry – for not beating him harder! – (*To Smuggler*.) Well, my dear, you shall come at night, and I'll make you amends!

Here Sir Harry takes snush.

SMUGGLER.

Madam, I will have amends before I leave the place. – Sir, how durst you use me thus?

SIR HARRY.

Sir!

SMUGGLER.

Sir, I say that I will have satisfaction!

SIR HARRY.

With all my heart!

Throws snush into his eyes.

SMUGGLER.

Oh, murder! blindness! fire! – Oh, madam! madam! get me some water! water! fire! fire! water!

Exit with Lady Lurewell.

SIR HARRY.

How pleasant is resenting an injury without passion! 'tis the beauty of revenge!
Let statesmen plot, and under business groan,
And settling public quiet lose their own;
Let soldiers drudge and fight for pay or fame,
For when they're shot, I think 'tis much the same.
Let scholars vex their brains with mood and tense,
And mad with strength of reason, fools commence,
Losing their wits in searching after sense;
Their *summum bonum* they must toil to gain,
And seeking pleasure, spend their life in pain.
I make the most of life, no hour misspend,
Pleasure's the means, and pleasure is my end.
No spleen, no trouble, shall my time destroy;
Life's but a span, I'll every inch enjoy.

Exit.

ACT THREE

Scene One

The Street. Enter Standard and Vizard,

STANDARD.

I bring him word where she lodged! I, the civillest rival in the world! – 'tis impossible!

VIZARD.

I shall urge it no farther, sir. I only thought, sir, that my character in the world might add authority to my words, without so many repetitions.

STANDARD.

Pardon me, dear Vizard; our belief struggles hard, before it can be brought to yield to the disadvantage of what we love: 'tis so great an abuse to our judgment, that it makes the faults of our choice our own failing. – But what said Sir Harry?

VIZARD.

He pitied the poor credulous colonel; laughed heartily; flew away with all the raptures of a bridegroom, repeating these lines:
A mistress ne'er can pall her lover's joys,
Whose wit can whet whene'er her beauty cloys.

STANDARD.

A mistress ne'er can pall! – by all my wrongs, he whores her! and I'm made their property. Vengeance! – Vizard, you must carry a note for me to Sir Harry.

VIZARD.

What! a challenge! I hope you don't design to fight?

STANDARD.

What! wear the livery of my King, and pocket an affront! – 'Twere an abuse to his Sacred Majesty! A soldier's sword, Vizard, should start of itself to redress its master's wrong!

VIZARD.

However, sir, I think it not proper for me to carry any such message between friends.

STANDARD.

I have ne'er a servant here; what shall I do?

VIZARD.

There's Tom Errand, the porter, that plies at the Blue Posts, and who knows Sir Harry and his haunts very well; you send a note by him.

TANDARD (*calls*).
No whispering now, nor telling of friends to prevent us. He

STANDARD (*calls*).
Here! you, friend.

IZARD.
I have now some business, and must take my leave; I would
advise you, nevertheless, against this affair.

TANDARD.
No whispering now, nor telling of friends to prevent us. He
that disappoints a man of an honourable revenge, may love
him foolishly like a wife, but never value him as a friend.

VIZARD (*aside*).
Nay, the devil take him that parts you, say!

Exit.

Enter Tom Errand, running.

ERRAND.
Did your honour call a porter?

STANDARD.
Is your name Tom Errand?

ERRAND.
People call me so, an't like your worship.

STANDARD.
D'ye know Sir Harry Wildair?

ERRAND.
Ay, very well, sir; he's one of my masters; many a round half-
crown have I had of his worship; he's newly come home from
France, sir.

STANDARD.
Go to the next coffee-house, and wait for me. –

Exit Errand.

O woman! woman!
How blest is man when favour'd by your smiles!
And how accursed when all those smiles are found
But wanton baits to soothe us to destruction!
Thus our chief joys with base allays are curst,
And our best things, when once corrupted, worst.

Exit.

Scene Two

The same. Enter Wildair, and Clincher Senior following.

CLINCHER SENIOR.
Sir, sir, sir! having some business of importance to communi-
cate to you, I would beg your attention to a trifling affair that I
would impart to you.

SIR HARRY.
What is your trifling business of importance, pray, sweet
sir?

CLINCHER SENIOR.
Pray, sir, are the roads deep between this and Paris?

SIR HARRY.
Why that question, sir?

CLINCHER SENIOR.
Because I design to go to the Jubilee, sir; I understand that
you are a traveller, sir; there is an air of travel in the tie of your
cravat, sir, there is indeed, sir. – I suppose, sir, you bought
this lace in Flanders?

SIR HARRY.
No, sir; this lace was made in Norway.

CLINCHER SENIOR.
Norway, sir!

SIR HARRY.
Yes, sir, of the shavings of deal boards.

CLINCHER SENIOR.
That's very strange now, faith! – Lace made of the shavings of
deal boards! Egad, sir, you travellers see very strange things
abroad! – very incredible things abroad, indeed! Well, I'll
have a cravat of that very same lace before I come home.

SIR HARRY.
But, sir, what preparations have you made for your
journey?

CLINCHER SENIOR.
A case of pocket-pistols for the bravoes – and a swimming-
girdle.

SIR HARRY.
Why these, sir?

CLINCHER SENIOR.
O Lord! sir, I'll tell you. Suppose us in Rome now; away goes
me, I, to some ball – for I'll be a mighty beau! Then, as I
said I go to some ball, or some bear-baiting – 'tis all one, you
know; then comes a fine Italian bona roba, and plucks me by

know; then comes a fine Italian bona roba, and plucks me by the sleeve, 'Seigniour Angle! Seigniour Angle!' – she's a very fine lady, observe that! – 'Seigniour Angle!' says she; 'Seigniora!' says I, and trips after her to the corner of the street – suppose it Russell Street here, or any other street; then, you know, I must invite her to the tavern – I can do no less. There, up comes her bravo; the Italian grows saucy, and I give him an English douse of the face – I can box, sir, box tightly; I was a 'prentice, sir. – But then, sir, he whips out his stiletto, and I whips out my bull-dog – slaps him through, trips down stairs, turns the corner of Russell Street again, and whips me into the ambassador's train, and there I'm safe as a beau behind the scenes!

SIR HARRY.
Was your pistol charged, sir?

CLINCHER SENIOR.
Only a brace of bullets, that's all, sir. – I design to shoot seven Italians a week, sir.

SIR HARRY.
Sir, you won't have provocation.

CLINCHER SENIOR.
Provocation, sir! – Zauns, sir! I'll kill any man for treading upon my corn! – and there will be a devilish throng of people there. – They say that all the princes in Italy will be there.

SIR HARRY.
And all the fops and fiddlers in Europe. – But the use of your swimming-girdle, pray, sir?

CLINCHER SENIOR.
O Lord, sir! that's easy. Suppose the ship cast away; – now, whilst other foolish people are busy at their prayers, I whips on my swimming-girdle, clasps a month's provision into my pockets, and sails me away like an egg in a duck's belly. – And harkee, sir; I have a new project in my head. Where d'ye think my swimming-girdle shall carry me upon this occasion? – 'tis a new project.

SIR HARRY.
Where, sir?

CLINCHER SENIOR.
To Civita Vecchia, faith and troth! and so save the charges of my passage. Well, sir, you must pardon me now, I'm going to see my mistress.

Exit.

SIR HARRY.
This fellow's an accomplished ass before he goes abroad. – Well! this Angelica has got into my heart, and I can't get her out of my head. I must pay her t'other visit.

Exit

Scene Three

Lady Darling's house. Angelica sola.

ANGELICA.
Unhappy state of woman! whose chief virtue is but ceremony, and our much boasted modesty but a slavish restraint. The strict confinement on our words makes our thoughts ramble more; and what preserves our outward fame, destroys our inward quiet. – 'Tis hard that love should be denied the privilege of hatred; that scandal and detraction should be so much indulged, yet sacred love and truth debarred our conversation.

Enter Lady Darling, Clincher Junior and Dicky.

LADY DARLING.
This is my daughter, cousin.

DICKY (*aside to him*).
Now, sir, remember your three scrapes.

CLINCHER JUNIOR (*saluting Angelica*).
One, two, three – (*Kisses her.*) your humble servant. – Was not that right, Dicky?

DICKY.
Ay, faith, sir; but why don't you speak to her?

CLINCHER JUNIOR.
I beg your pardon, Dicky, I know my distance. Would you have me speak to a lady at the first sight?

DICKY.
Ay, sir, by all means; the first aim is the surest.

CLINCHER JUNIOR.
Now for a good jest to make her laugh heartily. – By Jupiter Ammon, I'll go give her a kiss.

Goes toward her.
Enter Wildair, interposing.

SIR HARRY.
'Tis all to no purpose, I told you so before; your pitiful five

guineas will never do. – You may march, sir, for as far as five hundred pounds will go, I'll outbid you.

CLINCHER JUNIOR.

What the devil! the madman's here again.

LADY DARLING.

Bless me, cousin! what d'ye mean? Affront a gentleman of his quality in my house!

CLINCHER JUNIOR.

Quality! why, madam, I don't know what you mean by your madmen, and your beaux, and your quality. – They're all alike, I believe.

LADY DARLING.

Pray, sir, walk with me into the next room.

Exit, leading Clincher Junior, Dicky following.

ANGELICA.

Sir, if your conversation be no more agreeable than 'twas the last time, I would advise you to make it as short as you can.

SIR HARRY.

The offences of my last visit, madam, bore their punishment in the commission; and have made me as uneasy till I receive pardon as your ladyship can be till I sue for it.

ANGELICA.

Sir Harry, I did not well understand the offence, and must therefore proportion it to the greatness of your apology; if you would therefore have me think it light, take no great pains in an excuse.

SIR HARRY.

How sweet must be the lips that guard that tongue! – Then, madam, no more of past offences, let us prepare for joys to come; let this seal my pardon. – (*Kisses her hand.*) And this – (*Kisses again.*) initiate me to farther happiness.

ANGELICA.

Hold, sir, – one question, Sir Harry, and pray answer plainly: d'ye love me?

SIR HARRY.

Love you! does fire ascend? do hypocrites dissemble? usurers love gold, or great men flattery? Doubt these, then question that I love.

ANGELICA.

This shows your gallantry, sir, but not your love.

SIR HARRY.

View your own charms, madam, then judge my passion. Your beauty ravishes my eye, your voice my ear, and your touch has thrilled my melting soul.

ANGELICA.

If your words be real, 'tis in your power to raise an equal flame in me.

SIR HARRY.

Nay, then – I seize –

ANGELICA.

Hold, sir! 'tis also possible to make me detest and scorn you worse than the most profligate of your deceiving sex.

SIR HARRY (*aside*).

Ha! a very odd turn this. – (*Aloud.*) I hope, madam, you only affect anger, because you know your frowns are becoming.

ANGELICA.

Sir Harry, you being the best judge of your own designs, can best understand whether my anger should be real or dissembled. Think what strict modesty should bear, then judge of my resentments.

SIR HARRY.

Strict modesty should bear! Why, faith, madam, I believe the strictest modesty may bear fifty guineas, and I don't believe 'twill bear one farthing more.

ANGELICA.

What d'ye mean, sir?

SIR HARRY.

Nay, madam, what do you mean? If you go to that, I think now fifty guineas is a very fine offer for your strict modesty, as you call it.

ANGELICA.

'Tis more charitable, Sir Harry, to charge the impertinence of a man of your figure on his defect in understanding, than on his want of manners. – I'm afraid you're mad, sir.

SIR HARRY.

Why, madam, you're enough to make any man mad. 'Sdeath, are you not a –

ANGELICA.

What, sir?

SIR HARRY.

Why, a lady of – strict modesty, if you will have it so.

ANGELICA.

I shall never hereafter trust common report, which represented you, sir, a man of honour, wit, and breeding; for I find you very deficient in them all.

Exit.

SIR HARRY (*solus*).

Now I find that the strict pretences which the ladies of pleasure make to strict modesty, is the reason why those of quality are ashamed to wear it.

Enter Vizard.

VIZARD.

Ah, Sir Harry! have I caught you? Well, and what success?

SIR HARRY.

Success! 'Tis a shame for you young fellows in town here to let the wenches grow so saucy: I offered her fifty guineas, and she was in her airs presently. I could have had two countesses in Paris for half the money, and *Je vous remercie* into the bargain.

VIZARD.

Gone in her airs, say you? and did not you follow her?

SIR HARRY.

Whither should I follow her?

VIZARD.

Into her bedchamber, man: she went on purpose. You a man of gallantry, and not understand that a lady's best pleased when she puts on her airs, as you call it!

SIR HARRY.

She talked to me of strict modesty, and stuff.

VIZARD.

Certainly most women magnify their modesty, for the same reason that cowards boast their courage, because they have least on't. Come, come, Sir Harry, when you make your next assault, encourage your spirits with brisk burgundy; if you succed, 'tis well; if not, you have a fair excuse for your rudeness. I'll go in, and make your peace for what's past. – Oh, I had almost forgot – Colonel Standard wants to speak with you about some business.

SIR HARRY.

I'll wait upon him presently; d'ye know where he may be found?

VIZARD.

In the Piazza of Covent Garden, about an hour hence, I promised to see him, and there you may meet him. – (*Aside.*)

To have your throat cut. – (*Aloud.*) I'll go in and intercede for you.

SIR HARRY.

But no foul play with the lady, Vizard.

Exit

VIZARD.

No fair play, I can assure you.

Scene Four

The Street before Lady Lurewell's Lodgings. Clincher Senior and Lady Lurewell coquetting in the balcony. Enter below Colonel Standard.

STANDARD.

How weak is reason in disputes of love!
That daring reason which so oft pretends
To question works of high omnipotence,
Yet poorly truckles to our weakest passions,
And yields implicit faith to foolish love,
Paying blind zeal to faithless woman's eyes.
I've heard her falsehood with such pressing proofs,
That I no longer should distrust it.
Yet still my love would baffle demonstration,
And make impossibilities seem probable.

Looks up.

Ha! that fool too! what! stoop so low as that animal! – 'Tis true, women once fallen, like cowards in despair, will stick at nothing; there's no medium in their actions. They must be bright as angels, or black as fiends. But now for my revenge; I'll kick her cully before her face, call her a whore, curse the whole sex, and so leave her.

Goes in.

Scene Five

The scene changes to a dining room. Enter Lady Lurewell with Clincher Senior.

LADY LUREWELL.

O Lord, sir, 'tis my husband! What will become of you?

CLINCHER SENIOR.

Eh! your husband! oh, I shall be murdered! what shall I do! where shall I run! I'll creep into an oven; I'll climb up the chimney; I'll fly! I'll swim! – I wish to the Lord I were at the Jubilee now!

LADY LUREWELL.

Can't you think of anything, sir?

Enter Tom Errand.

What do you want, sir?

ERRAND.

Madam, I am looking for Sir Harry Wildair; I saw him come in here this morning, and did imagine he might be here still.

LADY LUREWELL.

A lucky hit! – Here, friend, change clothes with this gentle-man, quickly; strip!

CLINCHER SENIOR.

Ay, ay, quickly, strip! I'll give you half-a-crown. Come here: so.

They change clothes.

LADY LUREWELL (*to Clincher*).

Now slip you downstairs, and wait at the door till my husband be gone.

Exit Clincher.

And get you in there till I call you. (*Puts Errand into the next room.*)

Enter Standard.

Oh, sir! are you come? I wonder, sir, how you have the confidence to approach me after so base a trick!

STANDARD.

Oh, madam, all your artifices won't prevail.

LADY LUREWELL.

Nay, sir, your artifices won't avail. I thought, sir, that I gave you caution enough against troubling me with Sir Harry Wildair's company when I sent his letters back by you; yet you, forsooth, must tell him where I lodged, and expose me again to his impertinent courtship.

STANDARD.

I expose you to his courtship!

LADY LUREWELL.

I'll lay my life you'll deny it now. Come, come, sir; a pitiful lie is as scandalous to a red coat as an oath to a black. Did not Sir Harry himself tell me that he found out by you where I lodged?

STANDARD.

You're all lies! First, your heart is false, your eyes are double; one look belies another; and then your tongue does contradict them all. Madam, I see a little devil just now hammering out a lie in your pericranium.

LADY LUREWELL (*aside*).

As I hope for mercy, he's in the right on't – (*Aloud.*) Hold, sir, you have got the playhouse cant upon your tongue, and think that wit may privilege your railing; but I must tell you, sir, that what is satire upon the stage is ill manners here.

STANDARD.

What is feigned upon the stage, is here in reality real false-hood. Yes, yes, madam; I exposed you to the courtship of your fool Clincher too: I hope your female wiles will impose that upon me also –

LADY LUREWELL.

Clincher! nay, now you're stark mad. I know no such person.

STANDARD.

Oh, woman in perfection! not know him! 'Slife, madam, can my eyes, my piercing jealous eyes, be so deluded? Nay, madam, my nose could not mistake him; for I smelt the fop by his pulvilio from the balcony down to the street.

LADY LUREWELL.

The balcony! ha, ha, ha! the balcony! I'll be hanged but he has mistaken Sir Harry Wildair's footman, with a new French livery, for a beau.

STANDARD.

'Sdeath, madam, what is there in me that looks like a cully? Did I not see him?

LADY LUREWELL.

No, no, you could not see him; you're dreaming, Colonel. Will you believe your eyes, now that I have rubbed them open? – Here, you friend! (*Calls.*)

Re-enter Errand in Clincher's clothes.

STANDARD.

This is illusion all; my eyes conspire against themselves! 'tis legerdemain!

LADY LUREWELL.

Legerdemain! Is that all your acknowledgment for your rude behaviour? Or, what a curse is it to love as I do! But don't presume too far, sir, on my affection; for such ungenerous usage will soon return my tired heart. – (*To Errand.*) Begone, sir, to your impertinent master, and tell him I shall never be at leisure to receive any of his troublesome visits. – Send to me to know when I should be at home! – Begone, sir! – I am sure he has made me an unfortunate woman. (*Weeps.*)

Exit Errand.

STANDARD.
Nay, then there is no certainty in Nature; and truth is only falsehood well disguised.

LADY LUREWELL.
Sir, had not I owned my fond foolish passion, I should not have been subject to such unjust suspicions: but 'tis an ungrateful return. (*Weeping.*)

STANDARD (*aside*).
Now, where are all my firm resolves? I will believe her just. My passion raised my jealousy; then why mayn't love be blind in finding faults as in excusing them? – (*Aloud.*) I hope, madam, you'll pardon me, since jealousy, that magnified my suspicion, is as much the effect of love as my easiness in being satisfied.

LADY LUREWELL.
Easiness in being satisfied! You men have got an insolent way of extorting pardon by persisting in your faults. No, no, sir, cherish your suspicions, and feed upon your jealousy: 'tis fit meat for your squeamish stomach.
With me all women should this rule pursue:
Who thinks us false, should never find us true.

Exit in a rage.

Re-enter Clincher Senior.

CLINCHER SENIOR (*aside*).
Well, intriguing is the prettiest, pleasantest thing for a man of my parts! How shall we laugh at the husband when he is gone! – How sillily he looks! He's in labour of horns already: – to make a colonel a cuckold! 'Twill be rare news for the alderman.

STANDARD.
All this Sir Harry has occasioned; but he's brave, and will afford me just revenge. – Oh this is the porter I sent the challenge by. – Well, sir, have you found him?

CLINCHER SENIOR (*aside*).
What the devil does he mean now?

STANDARD.
Have you given Sir Harry the note, fellow?

CLINCHER SENIOR.
The note! – what note?

STANDARD.
The letter, blockhead! which I sent by you to Sir Harry Wildair. Have you seen him?

CLINCHER SENIOR (*aside*).
O Lord! what shall I say now? – (*Aloud.*) Seen him? – yes, sir – no, sir. – I have, sir – I have not, sir.

STANDARD.
The fellow's mad! Answer me directly, sirrah, or I'll break your head!

CLINCHER SENIOR.
I know Sir Harry very well, sir; but as, to the note, sir, I can't remember a word on't: truth is, I have a very bad memory.

STANDARD.
Oh, sir, I'll quicken your memory! (*Strikes him.*)

CLINCHER SENIOR.
Zauns, sir, hold! I did give him the note.

STANDARD.
And what answer?

CLINCHER SENIOR.
I mean, sir, I did not give him the note.

STANDARD.
What! d'ye banter, rascal? (*Strikes him again.*)

CLINCHER SENIOR.
Hold, sir! hold! – He did send an answer.

STANDARD.
What was't, villain?

CLINCHER SENIOR.
Why, truly, sir, I have forgot it: I told you that I had a very treacherous memory.

STANDARD.
I'll engage you shall remember me this month, rascal.

Beats him off and exit.
Re-enter Lady Lurewell, with Parly.

LADY LUREWELL.
Fort bon! fort bon! fort bon! – this is better than I expected; but fortune still helps the industrious.

Re-enter Clincher Senior.

CLINCHER SENIOR.

Ah, the devil take all intriguing, say I! and him who first invented canes! That cursed colonel has got such a knack of beating his men, that he has left the mark of a collar of bandoleers about my shoulder.s

LADY LUREWELL.

Oh, my poor gentleman! and was it beaten?

CLINCHER SENIOR.

Yes, I have been beaten: but where's my clothes? my clothes?

LADY LUREWELL.

What! you won't leave me so son, my dear, will ye?

CLINCHER SENIOR.

Will ye! – If ever I peep into a colonel's tent again, may I be forced to run the gauntlet! – But my clothes, madam.

LADY LUREWELL.

I sent the porter downstairs with them, did you not meet him?

CLINCHER SENIOR.

Meet him! no, not I.

PARLY.

No? He went out of the back door, and is run clear away, I'm afraid.

CLINCHER SENIOR.

Gone, say you? and with my clothes? my fine Jubilee clothes! – Oh, the rogue! the thief! – I'll have him hanged for murder. But how shall I get home in this pickle?

PARLY.

I'm afraid, sir, the colonel will be back presently; for he dines at home.

CLINCHER SENIOR.

Oh, then I must sneak off! – was ever man so managed! to have his coat well thrashed, and lose his coat too?

Exit

LADY LUREWELL.

Thus the noble poet spoke truth: –
Nothing suits worse with vice than want of sense:
Fools are still wicked at their own expense.

PARLY.

Methink, madam the injuries you have suffered by men must be very great to raise such heavy resentments against the whole sex.

LADY LUREWELL.

The greatest injury that woman could sustain: they robbed me of that jewel which, preserved, exalts our sex almost to angels; but destroyed, debases us below the worst of brutes – mankind.

PARLY.

But I think, madam, your anger should be only confined to the author of your wrongs.

LADY LUREWELL.

The author! – Alas! I know him not; which makes my wrongs the greater.

PARLY.

Not know him! 'tis odd, madam, that a man should rob you of that same jewel you mentioned, and you not know him!

LADY LUREWELL.

Leave trifling! – 'tis a subject that always sours my temper. But since, by thy faithful service, I have some reason to confide in your secrecy, hear the strange relation. Some twelve years ago I lived at my father's house in Oxfordshire, blest with innocence, the ornamental but weak guard of blooming beauty. I was then just fifteen, an age oft fatal to the female sex: – our youth is tempting, our innocence credulous, romances moving, love powerful, and men are – villains! Then it happened, that three young gentlemen, from the university, coming into the country, and being benighted, and strangers, called at my father's: he was very glad of their company, and offered them the entertainment of his house.

PARLY.

Which they accepted, no doubt. – Oh! these strolling collegians are never abroad but upon some mischief!

LADY LUREWELL.

They had some private frolic or design in their heads, as appeared by their not naming one another; which my father perceiving, out of civility, made no inquiry into their affairs. Two of them had a heavy, pedantic, university air, a sort of disagreeable scholastic boorishness in their behaviour; but the third! –

PARLY.

Ay, the third, madam! – the third of all things, they say, is very critical.

LADY LUREWELL.

He was – but, in short, nature cut him out for my undoing! He seemed to be about eighteen.

PARLY.

A fit match for your fifteen as could be.

LADY LUREWELL.

He had a genteel sweetness in his face, a graceful comeliness in his person, and his tongue was fit to soothe soft innocence to ruin. His very looks were witty, and his expressive eyes spoke softer, prettier things, than words could frame.

PARLY.

There will be mischief by-and-bye; I never heard a woman talk so much of eyes but there were tears presently after.

LADY LUREWELL.

His discourse was directed to my father, but his looks to me. After supper, I went to my chamber, and read Cassandra; then went to bed, and dreamt of him all night; rose in the morning, and made verses: so fell desperately in love. My father was well pleased with his conversation, that he begged their company next day; they consented; and next night, Parly –

PARLY.

Ay, next night, madam, – next night (I'm afraid) was a night indeed.

LADY LUREWELL.

He bribed my maid, with his gold, out of her honesty; and me, with his rhetoric, out of my honour. She admitted him to my chamber, and there he vowed, and swore, and wept, and sighed – and conquered. (*Weeps.*)

PARLY.

Alack-a-day, poor fifteen. (*Weeps.*)

LADY LUREWELL.

He swore that he would come down from Oxford in a fortnight, and marry me.

PARLY (*aside*).

The old bait! the old bait! – I was cheated just so myself. – (*Aloud.*) But had not you the wit to know his name all this while?

LADY LUREWELL.

Alas! what wit had innocence like mine? He told me, that he was under an obligation to his companions of concealing himself then, but that he would write to me in two days, and let me know his name and quality. After all the binding oaths of constancy, joining hands, exchanging hearts, I gave him a ring with this motto, 'Love and Honour'. Then we parted; but I never saw the dear deceiver more.

PARLY.

No, nor never will, I warrant you.

LADY LUREWELL.

I need not tell my griefs, which my father's death made a fair pretence for; he left me sole heiress and executrix to three thousand pounds a year. At last, my love for this single dissembler turned to a hatred of the whole sex; and, resolving to divert my melancholy, and make my large fortune subservient to my pleasure and revenge I went to travel, where, in most Courts of Europe, I have done some execution. Here I will play my last scene; then retire to my country house, live solitary, and die a penitent.

PARLY.

But don't you still love this dear dissembler?

LADY LUREWELL.

Most certainly: 'tis love of him that keeps my anger warm, representing the baseness of mankind full in view, and makes my resentments work. – We shall have that old impotent lecher Smuggler here tonight; I have a plot to swinge him, and his precise nephew Vizard.

PARLY.

I think, madam, you manage everybody that comes in your way.

LADY LUREWELL.

No, Parly; those men whose pretensions I found just and honourable, I fairly dismissed, by letting them know my firm resolutions never to marry. But those villains that would attempt my honour, I've seldom failed to manage.

PARLY.

What d'ye think of the colonel, madam? I suppose his designs are honourable.

LADY LUREWELL.

That man's a riddle; there's something of honour in his temper that pleases: I'm sure he loves me too, because he's soon jealous, and soon satisfied. But he's a man still. When I once tried his pulse about marriage, his blood ran as low as a coward's. He swore, indeed, that he loved me, but could not marry me forsooth, because he was engaged elsewhere. So poor a pretence made me disdain his passion, which otherwise might have been uneasy to me. But hang him, I have teased him enough. Besides, Parly, I begin to be tired of my revenge. – But this 'buss an guinea' I must maul once more: I'll hansel his woman's clothes for him! Go, get me pen and ink; I must write to Vizard too.

Exit Parly.

Fortune this once assist me as before,
Two such machines can never work in vain,
As thy propitious wheel, and my projecting brain.

Exit.

ACT FOUR

Scene One

Covent Garden. Wildair and Standard meeting

STANDARD.
I thought, Sir Harry, to have met you ere this in a more convenient place; but since my wrongs were without ceremony, my revenge shall be so too. Draw, sir!

SIR HARRY.
Draw, sir? What shall I draw?

STANDARD.
Come, come, sir, I like your facetious humour well enough; it shows courage and unconcern. I know you brave; and therefore use you thus. Draw your sword.

SIR HARRY.
Nay, to oblige you, I will draw; but the devil take me if I fight! – Perhaps, Colonel, this is the prettiest blade you have seen.

STANDARD.
I doubt not but the arm is good; and therefore think both worthy my resentment. Come, sir.

SIR HARRY.
But prithee, Colonel, dost think that I am such a madman as to send my soul to the devil and my body to the worms upon every fool's errand?

STANDARD.
I hope you're no coward, sir.

SIR HARRY.
Coward, sir! I have eight thousand pounds a year, sir.

STANDARD.
You fought in Flanders to my knowledge.

SIR HARRY.
Ay, for the same reason that I wore a red coat, because 'twas fashionable.

STANDARD.
Sir, you fought a French count in Paris.

SIR HARRY.
True, sir; he was a beau like myself. Now you're a soldier, Colonel, and fighting's your trade; and I think it downright madness to contend with any man in his profession.

STANDARD.

Come, sir, no more dallying: I shall take very unseemly methods if you don't show yourself a gentleman.

SIR HARRY.

A gentleman! why there again now? A gentleman! I tell you once more, Colonel, that I am a baronet, and have eight thousand pounds a year. I can dance, sing, ride, fence, understand the languages. Now, I can't conceive how running you through the body should contribute one jot more to my gentility. But pray, Colonel, I had forgot to ask you: what's the quarrel?

STANDARD.

A woman, sir.

SIR HARRY.

Then I put up my sword. – Take her.

STANDARD.

Sir, my honour's concerned.

SIR HARRY.

Nay, if your honour be concerned with a woman, get it out of her hands as soon as you can. An honourable lover is the greatest slave in nature; some will say, the greatest fool. Come, come, Colonel, this is something about the Lady Lurewell, I warrant; I can give you satisfaction in that affair.

STANDARD.

Do so then immediately.

SIR HARRY.

Put up your sword first; you know I dare fight: but I had much rather make you a friend than an enemy. I can assure you, this lady will prove too hard for one of your temper. You have too much honour, too much in conscience, to be a favourite with the ladies.

STANDARD.

I am assured, sir, she never gave you any encouragement.

SIR HARRY.

A man can never hear reason with a sword in his hand. Sheathe your weapon; and then if I don't satify you, sheathe it in my body.

STANDARD.

Give me but demonstration of her granting you any favour, and 'tis enough.

SIR HARRY.

Will you take my word?

STANDARD.

Pardon me, sir, I cannot.

SIR HARRY.

Will you believe your own eyes?

STANDARD.

'Tis ten to one whether I shall or no; they have deceived me already.

SIR HARRY.

That's hard. – But some means I shall devise for your satisfaction. We must fly this place, else that cluster of mob will overwhelm us.

Exeunt.

Enter Mob, Tom Errand's wife hurrying in Clincher Senior in Errand's clothes.

WIFE.

Oh, the villain! the rogue! he has murdered my husband: ah, my poor Timothy! (*Crying.*).

CLINCHER SENIOR.

Dem your Timothy! – Your husband has murdered me, woman; for he has carried away my fine Jubilee clothes.

WIFE.

Ay, you cut-throat, have you not got his clothes upon your back there? – Neighbours, don't you know poor Timothy's coat and apron?

MOB.

Ay, ay, 'tis the same.

1 MOB.

What shall we do with him, neighbours?

2 MOB.

We'll pull him in pieces.

1 MOB.

No, no; then we may be hanged for murder: but we'll drown him.

CLINCHER SENIOR.

Ah, good people, pray don't drown me; for I never learned to swim in all my life. – Ah, this plaguy intriguing!

MOB.

Away with him! away with him to the Thames!

CLINCHER SENIOR.

Oh, if I had but my swimming girdle now!

Enter Constable.

CONSTABLE.

Hold, neighbours! I command the peace.

WIFE.

Oh, Mr Constable, here's a rogue that has murdered my husband, and robbed him of his clothes.

CONSTABLE.

Murder and robbery! then he must be a gentleman. – Hands off there! he must not be abused. – Give an account of yourself: are you a gentleman?

CLINCHER SENIOR.

No, sir, I am a beau.

CONSTABLE.

Then you have killed nobody, I'm persuaded. How came you by these clothes, sir?

CLINCHER SENIOR.

You must know, sir, that walking along, sir, I don't know how, sir, I can't tell where, sir; and – so the porter and I changed clothes, sir.

CONSTABLE.

Very well. The man speaks reason and like a gentleman.

WIFE.

But pray, Mr Constable, ask him how he changed clothes with him.

CONSTABLE.

Silence, woman! and don't disturb the court. – Well, sir, how did you change clothes?

CLINCHER SENIOR.

Why, sir, he pulled off my coat, and I drew off his; so I put on his coat, and he puts on mine.

CONSTABLE.

Why, neighbours, I don't find that he's guilty. Search him; and if he carries no arms about him, we'll let him go.

They search his pockets, and pull out his pistols.

CLINCHER SENIOR.

O gemini! my Jubilee pistols!

CONSTABLE.

What, a case of pistols! then the case is plain. – Speak, what are you, sir? whence came you, and whither go you?

CLINCHER SENIOR.

Sir, I came from Russell Street, and am going to the Jubilee.

WIFE.

You shall go to the gallows, you rogue!

CONSTABLE.

Away with him! away with him to Newgate, straight!

CLINCHER SENIOR.

I shall go to the Jubilee now, indeed.

Exeunt

Re-enter Wildair and Standard.

SIR HARRY.

In short, Colonel, 'tis all nonsense. Fight for a woman! – Hard by is the lady's house; if you please we'll wait on her together: you shall draw your sword, I'll draw my snuff-box: you shall produce your wounds received in war, I'll relate mine by Cupid's dart: you shall look big, I'll ogle: you shall swear, I'll sight: you shall sa! sa! and I'll coupee: and if she flies not to my arms like a hawk to its perch, my dancing-master deserves to be damned!

STANDARD.

With the generality of women, I grant you, these arts may prevail.

SIR HARRY.

Generality of women! why, there again you're out. They're all alike, sir; I never heard of any one that was particular, but one.

STANDARD.

Who was she, pray?

SIR HARRY.

Penelope, I think, she's called; and that's a poetical story too. When will you find a poet in our age make a woman so chaste?

STANDARD.

Well, Sir Harry, your facetious humour can disguise falsehood, and make calumny pass for satire. But you have promised me ocular demonstration that she favours you: make that good, and I shall then maintain faith and female to be as inconsistent as truth and falsehood.

SIR HARRY.

Nay, by what you have told me, I am satisfied that she imposes on us all; and Vizard, too, seems what I still suspected him; but his honesty once mistrusted, spoils his knavery. – But will you be convinced, if our plot succeeds?

STANDARD.

I rely on your word and honour, Sir Harry; which if I doubted, my distrust would cancel the obligation of their security.

SIR HARRY.

Then meet me half-an-hour hence at the Rummer. You must oblige me by taking a hearty glass with me toward the fitting me out for a certain project which this night I undertake.

STANDARD.

I guess by the preparation that woman's the design.

SIR HARRY.

Yes, faith. – I am taken dangerously ill with two foolish maladies, modesty and love; the first I'll cure with burgundy, and my love by a night's lodging with the damsel. A sure remedy. *Probatum est!*

STANDARD.

I'll certainly meet you, sir.

Exeunt severally.

Scene Two

The same. Enter Clincher Junior and Dicky.

CLINCHER JUNIOR.

Ah, Dicky, this London is a sad place! a sad vicious place! I wish that I were in the country again. – And this brother of mine! I'm sorry he's so great a rake: I had rather see him dead than see him thus.

DICKY.

Ay, sir, he'll spend his whole estate at this same Jubilee. Who d'ye think lives at this same Jubilee?

CLINCHER JUNIOR.

Who, pray?

DICKY.

The Pope.

CLINCHER JUNIOR.

The devil he does! My brother go to the place where the Pope dwells! he's bewitched sure.

Enter Tom Errand in Clincher Senior's clothes.

DICKY.

Indeed I believe he is, for he's strangely altered.

CLINCHER JUNIOR.

Altered! why he looks like a Jesuit already.

ERRAND (*aside*).

This lace will sell. What a blockhead was the fellow to trust me with his coat! If I can get across the Garden, down to the water side, I'm pretty, secure.

CLINCHER JUNIOR.

Brother! – Alaw! O gemini! are you my brother?

DICKY.

I seize you in the king's name, sir.

ERRAND (*aside*).

O Lord! should this prove some parliament man now!

CLINCHER JUNIOR.

Speak, you rogue, what are you?

ERRAND.

A poor porter, sir, and going of an errand.

DICKY.

What errand? speak, you rogue.

ERRAND.

A fool's errand, I'm afraid.

CLINCHER JUNIOR.

Who sent you?

ERRAND.

A beau, sir.

DICKY.

No, no, the rogue has murdered your brother, and stripped him of his clothes.

CLINCHER JUNIOR.

Murdered my brother! O crimini! O my poor Jubilee brother! – Stay, by Jupiter Ammon, I'm heir though! – Speak, sirrah, have you killed him? Confess that you have killed him, and I'll give you half-a-crown.

ERRAND.

Who, I, sir? Alack-a-day, sir, I never killed any man but a carrier's horse once.

CLINCHER JUNIOR.

Then you shall certainly be hanged; but confess that you killed him, and we'll let you go.

ERRAND (*aside*).

Telling the truth hangs a man, but confessing a lie can do no harm; besides, if the worst comes to the worst, I can but deny it again. – (*Aloud.*) Well, sir, since I must tell you, I did kill him.

CLINCHER JUNIOR.

Here's your money, sir: – but are you sure you killed him dead?

ERRAND.

Sir, I'll swear it before any judge in England.

DICKY.

But are you sure that he's dead in law?

ERRAND.

Dead in law! I can't tell whether he be dead in law: but he's dead as a door-nail; for I gave him seven knocks on the head with a hammer.

DICKY.

Then you have the estate by the statute. Any man that's knocked o' th' head is dead in law.

CLINCHER JUNIOR.

But are you sure he was *compos mentis* when he was killed?

ERRAND.

I suppose he was, sir; for he told me nothing to the contrary afterwards.

CLINCHER JUNIOR.

Hey! then I go to the Jubilee. – Strip, sir, strip! by Jupiter Ammon, strip!

Exchanges clothes with Tom Errand.

DICKY.

Ah! don't swear, sir.

CLINCHER JUNIOR.

Swear, sir! Zoons, han't I got the estate, sir? Come, sir, now I'm in mourning for my brother.

ERRAND.

I hope you'll let me go now, sir –

CLINCHER JUNIOR.

Yes, yes, sir; but you must first do me the favour to swear postively before a magistrate that you killed him dead, that I may enter upon the estate without any trouble. By Jupiter Ammon, all my religion's gone since I put on these fine clothes! – Hey! call me a coach somebody.

ERRAND.

Ay, master, let me go, and I'll call one immediately.

CLINCHER JUNIOR.

No, no, Dicky, carry this spark before a justice, and when he has made oath, you may discharge him.

Exeunt Dicky and Errand.

And I'll go see Angelica. Now that I'm an elder brother, I'll court, and swear, and rant, and rake, and go to the Jubilee with the best of them.

Exit.

Scene Three

A room in Lady Lurewell's house. Enter Lady Lurewell and Parly.

LADY LUREWELL.

Are you sure that Vizard had my letter?

PARLY.

Yes, yes, madam; one of your ladyship's footmen gave it to him in the Park, and he told the bearer, with all transports of joy, that he would be punctual to a minute.

LADY LUREWELL.

Thus most villains, sometime or other, are punctual to their ruin; and hypocrisy, by imposing on the world, at last deceives itself. Are all things prepared for his reception?

PARLY.

Exactly to your ladyship's order; the alderman too, is just come, dressed and cooked up for iniquity.

LADY LUREWELL.

Then he has got woman's clothes on?

PARLY.

Yes, madam, and has passed upon the family for your nurse.

LADY LUREWELL.

Convey him into that closet, and put out the candles, and tell him I'll wait on him presently. –

As Parly goes to put out the candles, somebody knocks.

This must be some clown without manners, or a gentleman above ceremony. – Who's there?

SONG

SIR HARRY (*without*).
　Thus Damon knock'd at Celia's door,
　He sigh'd, and begg'd, and wept, and swore;
　　The sign was so;

Knocks.

　　She answer'd, no,
　　No, no, no.

Knocks thrice.

　Again he sigh'd, again he pray'd; –
　'No, Damon, no, I am afraid'
　Consider, Damon, I'm a maid,
　　Consider; no,
　　I am a maid.
　　No, no, no.'

　At last his sighs and tears made way,
　She rose, and softly turned the key;
　'Come in,' said she, 'but do not stay.
　　I may conclude
　　You will be rude,
　　But, if you are, you may.'

Exit Parly.

Wildair enters.

LADY LUREWELL.
　'Tis too early for serenading, Sir Harry.

SIR HARRY.
　Wheresoever love is, there music is proper; there's an harmonious consent in their natures, and, when rightly joined, they make up the chorus of earthly happiness.

LADY LUREWELL.
　But, Sir Harry, what tempest drives you here at this hour?

SIR HARRY.
　No tempest, madam, but as fair weather as ever enticed a citizen's wife to cuckold her husband in fresh air: – love, madam. (*Taking her by the hand.*)

LADY LUREWELL.
　As pure and white as angels' soft desires. – Is't not so?

SIR HARRY.
　Fierce as when ripe consenting beauty fires.

LADY LUREWELL (*aside*).
　O villain! What privilege has man to our destruction, that thus they hunt our ruin?

Wildair drops a ring, she takes it up.

　If this be a love-token your mistress's favours hang very loose about you, sir.

SIR HARRY.
　I can't justly, madam, pay your trouble of taking it up by anything but desiring you to wear it.

LADY LUREWELL.
　You gentlemen have the cunningest ways of playing the fool and are so industrious in your profuseness! Speak seriously, am I beholden to chance or design for this ring?

SIR HARRY.
　To design, upon my honour, (*Aside.*) and I hope my design will succeed.

LADY LUREWELL (*singing*).
　And what shall I give you for such a fine thing?

SIR HARRY (*singing*).
　You'll give me another, you'll give me another fine thing.

LADY LUREWELL.
　Shall I be free with you, Sir Harry?

SIR HARRY.
　With all my heart, madam, so I may be free with you.

LADY LUREWELL.
　Then, plainly, sir, I shall beg the favour to see you some other time, for at this very minute I have two lovers in the house.

SIR HARRY.
　Then, to be as plain, I must be gone this minute, for I must see another mistress within these two hours.

LADY LUREWELL.
　Frank and free.

SIR HARRY.
　As you with me. – Madam, your most humble servant.

Exit.

LADY LUREWELL.
　Nothing can disturb his humour. – Now for my merchant and Vizard.

Exit, and takes the candles with her.

Re-enter Parley, leading in Smuggler, dressed in woman's clothes.

PARLY.

This way, Mr Alderman.

SMUGGLER.

Well, Mrs Parly, I'm obliged to you for this trouble; here are a couple of shillings for you. Times are hard, very hard indeed, but next time I'll steal a pair of silk stockings from my wife, and bring them to you. – What are you fumbling about my pockets for?

PARLY.

Only settling the plaits of your gown. Here, sir, get into this closet, and my lady will wait on you presently.

Puts him into the closet, runs out, and returns with Vizard.

VIZARD.

Where wouldst thou lead me, my dear auspicious little pilot?

PARLY.

You're almost in port, sir; my lady's in the closet, and will come out to you immediately.

VIZARD.

Let me thank thee as I ought. (*Kisses.*)

PARLY (*aside*).

Psha! who has hired me best – a couple of shillings or a couple of kisses?

Exit.

VIZARD.

Propitious darkness guides the lover's steps, and night that shadows outward sense, lights up our inward joy. Night! the great awful ruler of mankind, which like the Persian monarch, hides its royalty to raise the veneration of the world. Under thy easy reign dissemblers may speak truth; all slavish forms and ceremonies laid aside, and generous villany may act without constraint.

SMUGGLER (*peeping out of the closet*).

Bless me! what voice is this?

VIZARD.

Our hungry appetites, like the wild beasts of prey, now scour abroad to gorge their craving maws; the pleasure of hypocrisy, like a chained lion once broke loose, wildly indulges its new freedom, ranging through all unbounded joys.

SMUGGLER (*aside*).

My nephew's voice, and certainly possessed with an evil spirit; he talks as profanely as an actor possessed with a poet.

VIZARD.

Ha! I hear a voice. – Madam – my life, my happiness, where are you, madam

SMUGGLER (*aside*).

Madam! He takes me for a woman too; I'll try him. – (*Aloud.*) Where have you left your sanctity, Mr Vizard?

VIZARD.

Talk no more of that ungrateful subject – I left it where it has only business, with daylight; 'tis needless to wear a mask in the dark.

SMUGGLER (*aside*).

O the rogue, the rogue! – (*Aloud.*) The world takes you for a very sober, virtuous gentleman.

VIZARD.

Ay, madam, that adds security to all my pleasures. With me a cully-squire may squander his estate, and ne'er be thought a spendthrift: with me a holy elder may zealously be drunk, and toast his tuneful nose in sack, to make it hold forth clearer: but what is most my praise, the formal rigid she, that rails at vice and men, with me secures her loosest pleasures, and her strictest honour. She who with scornful mien and virtuous pride disdains the name of whore, with me can wanton, and laugh at the deluded world.

SMUGGLEY (*aside*).

How have I been deceived! – (*Aloud.*) Then you are very great among the ladies?

VIZARD.

Yes, madam: they know that, like a mole in the earth, I dig deep, but invisible; not like those fluttering noisy sinners, whose pleasure is the proclamation of their faults; those empty flashes who no sooner kindle, but they must blaze to alarm the world. – But come, madam, you delay our pleasures.

SMUGGLER (*aside*).

He surely takes me for the Lady Lurewell; she has made him an appointment too; but I'll be revenged of both. – (*Aloud.*) Well, sir, what are those you are so intimate with?

VIZARD.

Come, come, madam, you know very well – those who stand so high, that the vulgar envy even their crimes, whose figure adds privilege to their sin, and makes it pass unquestioned; fair, high, pampered females, whose speaking eyes and piercing voice would arm the statue of a Stoic, and animate his cold marble with the soul of an Epicure; all ravishing, lovely, soft, and kind, like you!

SMUGGLER (*aside*).
I am very lovely and soft indeed! you shall find me much harder than you imagine, friend! – (*Aloud.*) Well, sir, but I suppose your dissimulation has some other motive besides pleasure?

VIZARD.
Yes, madam, the honestest motive in the world – interest. You must know, madam, that I have an old uncle, Alderman Smuggler – you have seen him, I suppose?

SMUGGLER.
Yes, yes, I have some small acquaintance with him.

VIZARD.
'Tis the most knavish, precise, covetous old rogue that ever died of a gout.

SMUGGLER (*aside*).
Ah! the young son of a whore! – (*Aloud.*) Well, sir, and what of him?

VIZARD.
Hell hungers not more for wretched souls than he for ill-got pelf: and yet (what's wonderful) he that would stick at no profitable villainy himself, loves holiness in another. He prays all Sunday for the sins of the week past; he spends all dinner-time in too tedious graces; and what he designs a blessing to the meat, proves a curse to his family. He's the most –

SMUGGLER.
Well, well, sir, I know him very well.

VIZARD.
Then madam, he has a swinging estate, which I design to purchase as a saint and spend like a gentleman. He got it by cheating, and should lose it by deceit. By the pretence of my zeal and sobriety, I'll cozen the old miser one of these days out of a settlement and deed of conveyance –

SMUGGLER (*aside*).
It shall be a deed to convey you to the gallows, then, you young dog!

VIZARD.
And no sooner he's dead, but I'll rattle over his grave with a coach-and-six, to inform his covetous ghost how genteelly I spend his money.

SMUGGLER (*aside*).
I'll prevent you, boy; for I'll have my money buried with me.

VIZARD.
Bless me, madam! here's a light coming this way; I must fly immediately! When shall I see you, madam?

SMUGGLER.
Sooner than you expect, my dear!

VIZARD.
Pardon me, dear madam. I would not be seen for the world. I would sooner forfeit my life, nay, my pleasure, than my reputation.

Exit.

SMUGGLER.
Reputation! reputation! that poor word suffers a great deal. Well, thou art the most accomplished hypocrite that ever made a grave plodding face over a dish of coffee and a pipe of tobacco! He owes me for seven years' maintenance, and shall pay me by seven years' imprisonment; and when I die, I'll leave him to the fee-simple of a rope and a shilling! – Who are these! I begin to be afraid of some mischief. I wish that I were safe within the city liberties. – I'll hide myself. (*Stands close.*)

Enter Butler and Footmen with lights.

BUTLER.
I say, there are two spoons wanting, and I'll search the whole house. Two spoons will be no small gap in my quarter's wages.

FOOTMAN.
When did you miss them, James?

BUTLER.
Miss them? why, I miss them now; in short, they must be among you; and if you don't return them, I'll go to the cunning-man to-morrow morning; my spoons I want, and my spoons I will have.

FOOTMAN.
Come, come, search about. –

Search and discover Smuggler.

Ah! who's this?

BUTLER.
Hark'ee, good woman, what makes you hide yourself? what are you ashamed of?

SMUGGLER.

Ashamed of! – O Lord, sir! I'm an honest old woman that never was ashamed of anything.

BUTLER.

What are you? a midwife then? Speak, did not you see a couple of stray spoons in your travels?

SMUGGLER.

Stray spoons?

BUTLER.

Ay, ay, stray spoons; in short, you stole them, and I'll shake your old limbs to pieces if you don't deliver them presently.

SMUGGLER (*aside*).

Bless me, a reverend elder of seventy years old accused for petty larceny! – (*Aloud.*) Why, search me, good people search me; and if you find any spoons about me, you shall burn me for a witch.

BUTLER.

Ay, ay, we will search you, mistress.

They search and pull the spoons out of his pocket.

SMUGGLER.

Oh, the devil! the devil!

BUTLER.

Where? where is he? – Lord bless us! she is a witch in good earnest, maybe!

SMUGGLER.

Oh, it was some devil, some Covent Garden or St. James's devil that put them in my pocket!

BUTLER.

Ay, ay, you shall be hanged for a thief, burned for a witch, and then carted for a bawd. Speak, what are you?

Re-enter Lady Lurewell.

SMUGGLER.

I'm the Lady Lurewell's nurse.

LADY LUREWELL.

What noise is this?

BUTLER.

Here is an old succubus, madam, that has stole two silver spoons, and says she's your nurse.

LADY LUREWELL.

My nurse! Oh the impudent old jade! I never saw the withered creature before.

SMUGGLER (*aside*).

Then I'm finely caught! – (*Aloud.*) O madam, madam! don't you know me? don't you remember buss and guinea?

LADY LUREWELL.

Was ever such impudence! – I know thee! why, thou'rt as brazen as a bawd in the side-box. – Take her before a justice, and then to Newgate. Away!

SMUGGLER (*aside to Lady Lurewell*).

Oh! consider, madam, that I'm an alderman.

LADY LUREWELL (*aside to Smuggler*).

Consider, sir, that you're a compound of covetousness, hypocrisy, and knavery, and must be punished accordingly. You must be in petticoats, gouty monster, must ye! you must 'buss and guinea' too! you must tempt a lady's honour, old satyr! (*Aloud.*) Away with him!

Butler and Footmen hurry Smuggler off.

Still may our sex thus frauds of men oppose,
Still may our arts delude these tempting foes:
May honour rule, and never fall betray'd.
But vice be caught in nets for virtue laid.

ACT FIVE

Scene One

Lady Darling's House. Lady Darling and Angelica.

LADY DARLING.

Daughter, since you have to deal with a man of so peculiar a temper, you must not think the general arts of love can secure him; you may therefore allow such a courtier some encouragement extraordinary, without reproach to your modesty.

ANGELICA.

I am sensible, madam, that a formal nicety makes our modesty sit awkward, and appears rather a chain to enslave than bracelet to adorn us: it should show, when unmolested, easy and innocent as a dove, but strong and vigorous as a falcon when assaulted.

LADY DARLING.

I'm afraid, daughter, you mistake Sir Harry's gaiety for dishonour.

ANGELICA.

Though modesty, madam, may wink, it must not sleep, when powerful enemies are abroad. I must confess, that of all men's, I would not see Sir Harry Wildair's faults; nay, I could wrest his most suspicious words a thousand ways to make them look like honour. – But, madam, in spite of love, I must hate him, and curse those practices which taint our nobility, and rob all virtuous women of the bravest men.

LADY DARLING.

You must certainly be mistaken, Angelica; for I'm satisfied Sir Harry's designs are only to court and marry you.

ANGELICA.

His pretence, perhaps, was such; but women now, like enemies, are attacked; whether by treachery or fairly conquered, the glory of triumph is the same. Pray, madam, by what means were you made acquainted with his designs?

LADY DARLING.

Means, child! Why, my cousin Vizard, who, I'm sure, is your sincere friend, sent him. He brought me this letter from my cousin.

Gives her the letter, which she opens.

ANGELICA (*aside*).

Ha! Vizard! then I'm abused in earnest. Would Sir Harry, by his instigation, fix a base affront upon me? No, I can't suspect him of so ungenteel a crime. This letter shall trace the truth. – (*Aloud.*) My suspicions, madam, are much cleared; and I hope to satisfy your ladyship in my management when next I see Sir Harry.

Enter Footman.

FOOTMAN.

Madam, here's a gentleman below calls himself Wildair.

LADY DARLING.

Conduct him up. –

Exit Footman

Daughter, I won't doubt your discretion.

Exit

Enter Wildair.

SIR HARRY.

Oh, the delights of love and burgundy! – Madam, I have toasted your ladyship fifteen bumpers successively, and swallowed Cupids like loaches, to every glass.

ANGELICA.

And what then, sir?

SIR HARRY.

Why then, madam, the wine has got into my head, and the Cupids into my heart; and unless by quenching quick my flame, you kindly ease the smart, I'm a lost man, madam.

ANGELICA.

Drunkenness, Sir Harry, is the worst pretence a gentleman can make for rudeness: for the excuse is as scandalous as the fault. – Therefore, pray consider who you are so free with, sir; a woman of condition, that can call half-a-dozen footmen upon occasion.

SIR HARRY.

Nay, madam, if you have a mind to toss me in a blanket, half-a-dozen chambermaids would do better service. – Come, come, madam, though the wine makes me lisp, yet has it taught me to speak plainer. By all the dust of my ancient progenitors, I must this night quarter my coat-of-arms with yours.

ANGELICA.

Nay then – Who waits there? (*Calls.*)

Enter footmen.

Take hold of that madman, and bind him.

SIR HARRY.

Nay, then burgundy's the word, and slaughter will ensue.
Hold! – do you know, scoundrels, that I have been drinking
victorious burgundy? (*Draws.*)

FOOTMAN.

We know you're drunk, sir.

SIR HARRY.

Then, how have you the impudence, rascals, to assault a
gentleman with a couple of flasks of courage in his head?

FOOTMAN.

Sir, we must do as our young mistress commands us.

SIR HARRY.

Nay, then have among ye, dogs!

*Throws money among them; they scramble, and take it up. He,
pelting them out, shuts the door, and returns.*

Rascals! Poltroons! – I have charmed the dragon, and now the
fruit's my own.

ANGELICA.

Oh, the mercenary wretches! this was a plot to betray me.

SIR HARRY.

I have put the whole army to flight: and now take the general
prisoner. (*Laying hold of her.*)

ANGELICA.

I conjure you, sir, by the sacred name of honour, by your
dead father's name, and the fair reputation of your mother's
chastity, that you offer not the least offence! – Already you
have wronged me past redress.

SIR HARRY.

Thou art the most unaccountable creature!

ANGELICA.

What madness, Sir Harry, what wild dream of loose desire
could prompt you to attempt this baseness? View me well.
The brightness of my mind, methinks, should lighten
outwards, and let you see your mistake in my behaviour. I
think it shines with so much innocence in my face,
That it should dazzle all your vicious thoughts.
Think not I am defenceless 'cause alone.
Your very self is guard against yourself:
I'm sure, there's something generous in your soul;
My words shall search it out,
And eyes shall fire it for my own defence.

SIR HARRY (*mimicking*).

Tall ti dum, ti dum, tall ti didi, didum. – A million to one now
but this girl is just come flush from reading the 'Rival
Queens'. Egad, I'll at her in her own cant. – 'O my Statira! O
my angry dear! Turn thy eyes on me', – behold thy beau in
buskins.

ANGELICA.

Behold me, sir; view me with a sober thought, free from those
fumes of wine that throw a mist before your sight, and you
shall find that every glance from my reproaching eyes is arm'd
with sharp resentment, and with a virtuous pride that looks
dishonour dead.

SIR HARRY (*aside*).

This is the first whore in heroics that I have met with. –
(*Aloud.*) Look ye, madam, as to that slander particular of your
virtue, we sha'n't quarrel about it; you may be as virtuous as
any woman in England, if you please; you may say your
prayers all the time. – But pray, madam, be pleased to
consider what is this same virtue that you make such a mighty
noise about? Can your virtue bespeak you a front row in the
boxes? No; for the players can't live upon virtue. Can your
virtue keep you a coach and six? No, no, your virtuous
women walk a-foot. Can your virtue hire you a pew in a
church? Why, the very sexton will tell you, now. Can your
virtue stake for you at picquet? No. Then what business has a
woman with virtue? Come, come, madam, I offered you fifty
guineas: there's a hundred. – The devil! Virtuous still! Why,
'tis a hundred, five score, a hundred guineas.

ANGELICA.

O indignation!
Were I a man, you durst not use me thus;
But the mean, poor abuse you throw on me,
Reflects upon yourself!
Our sex still strikes an awe upon the brave,
And only cowards dare affront a woman.

SIR HARRY.

Affront! 'Sdeath, madam! a hundred guineas will set you up
at basset, a hundred guineas will furnish out your lodgings
with china; a hundred guineas will give you an air of quality; a
hundred guineas will buy you a rich escritoir for your billets-
doux, or a fine Common-Prayer-Book for your virtue. A
hundred guineas wil buy a hundred fine things, and fine
things are for fine ladies; and fine ladies are for fine gentlemen; and fine gentlemen are – egad, this burgundy makes a
man speak like an angel. – Come, come, madam, take it and
put it to what use you please.

ANGELICA.

I'll use it as I would the base unworthy giver – thus.

Throws down the purse and stamps upon it.

SIR HARRY.

I have no mind to meddle in State affairs; but these women will make me a parliament man 'spite of my teeth, on purpose to bring in a bill against their extortion. She tramples underfoot that deity which all the world adores. – Oh, the blooming pride of beautiful eighteen! Psha, I'll talk to her no longer; I'll make my markets with the old gentlewoman; she knows business better. – (*Goes to the door, and calls.*) Here, you friend, pray desire the old lady to walk in. – Hark'ee, by Gad, madam, I'll tell your mother.

Re-enter Lady Darling.

LADY DARLING.

Well, Sir Harry, and how d'ye like my daughter, pray?

SIR HARRY.

Like her, madam! – Hark'ee will you take it? – Why, faith, madam, take the money, I say, or egad, all's out.

ANGELICA.

All shall out. Sir, you're a scandal to the name of gentleman.

SIR HARRY.

With all my heart, madam. – In short, madam, your daughter has used me somewhat too familiarly, though I have treated her like a woman of quality.

LADY DARLING.

How, sir?

SIR HARRY.

Why, madam I have offered her a hundred guineas.

LADY DARLING.

A hundred guineas! upon what score?

SIR HARRY.

Upon what score! Lord! Lord! how these old women love to hear bawdy! Why, faith, madam, I have ne'er a *double-entendre* ready at present, but I'll sing you a song.
(*Sings.*)
Behold the goldfinches, tall al de rall,
And a man of my inches, tall al de rall;
You shall take 'em, believe me, tall al de rall,
If you will give me your – tall al de rall.
A modish minuet, madam, that's all.

LADY DARLING.

Sir, I don't understand you.

SIR HARRY (*aside*).

Ay, she will have it in plain terms. – (*Aloud.*) Then, madam in downright English, I offered your daughter a hundred guineas to

ANGELICA.

Hold, sir stop your abusive tongue! too loose for modest ears to bear. Madam, I did before suspect that his designs were base, now they're too plain; this knight, this mighty man of wit and humours, is made a tool to a knave: Vizard has sent him of a bully's errand, to affront a woman; but I scorn the abuse, and him that offered it.

LADY DARLING.

How, sir, come to affront us! D'ye know who we are, sir?

SIR HARRY.

Know who ye are? Why your daughter there is Mr Vizard's cousin, I suppose: – and for you, madam, – (*aside.*) now to call her procuress *à la mode France*, – (*Aloud.*) *J'estime votre occupation –*

LADY DARLING.

Pray, sir, speak English.

SIR HARRY (*aside*).

Then to define her office, *à la mode Londres!* – (*Aloud.*) I suppose your ladyship to be one of those civil, obliging, discreet old gentlewomen, who keep their visiting days for the entertainment of their presenting friends, whom they treat with imperial tea, a private room, and a pack of cards. Now I suppose you do understand me.

LADY DARLING.

This is beyond sufferance! But say, thou abusive man, what injury have you e'er received from me or mine thus to engage you in this scandalous aspersion?

ANGELICA.

Yes, sir, what cause, what motives, could induce you thus to debase yourself below your rank?

SIR HARRY.

Heyday! Now, dear Roxana, and you my fair Statira, be not so very heroic in your styles; Vizard's letter may resolve you, and answer all the impertinent questions you have made me.

BOTH WOMEN.

We appeal to that.

SIR HARRY.

And I'll stand to't; he read it to me, and the contents were pretty plain, I thought.

ANGELICA.

Here, sir, peruse it, and see how much we are injured, and you deceived.

SIR HARRY (*opening the letter*).

But hold, madam – (*To Lady Darling.*) before I read, I'll make some condition. Mr Vizard says here, that I won't scruple 30 or 40 pieces. Now, madam, if you have clapped in another cipher to the account, and make it three or four hundred, by Gad, I will not stand to't.

ANGELICA.

Now can't I tell whether disdain or anger be the most just resentment for this injury.

LADY DARLING.

The letter, sir, shall answer you.

SIR HARRY.

Well then! – (*Reads.*) 'Out of my earnest inclination to serve your ladyship, and my cousin Angelica' – Ay, ay, the very words, I can say it by heart – 'I have sent Sir Harry Wildair to court my cousin.' – What the devil's this? – Sent Sir Harry Wildair to court my cousin! – He read to me quite a different thing. – 'He's a gentleman of great parts and fortune' – He's a son of a whore, and a rascal! – 'And would make your daughter very happy (*Whistles.*) in a husband'. – Oh, poor Sir Harry! what have thy angry stars designed? (*Looks foolish, and hums a song.*)

ANGELICA.

Now, sir, I hope you need no instigation to redress our wrongs, since even the injury points the way.

LADY DARLING.

Think, sir, that our blood for many generations has run in the purest channel of unsullied honour.

SIR HARRY.

Ay, madam. (*Bows to her.*)

ANGELICA.

Consider what a tender blossom is female reputation, which the least air of foul detraction blasts.

SIR HARRY.

Yes, madam. (*Bows to Angelica.*)

LADY DARLING.

Call then to mind your rude and scandalous behaviour.

SIR HARRY.

Right, madam. (*Bows again.*)

ANGELICA.

Remember the base price you offered me.

> *Exit.*

SIR HARRY.

Very true, madam. – Was ever man so catechised?

LADY DARLING.

Then think that Vizard, villain Vizard, caused all this, yet lives. That's all, farewell!

> *Going.*

SIR HARRY.

Stay, madam, one word. Is there no other way to redress your wrongs, but by fighting?

LADY DARLING.

Only one, sir, which if you can think of, you may do; you know the buiness I entertained you for.

SIR HARRY.

I understand you, madam. –

Exit Lady Darling.

Here am I brought to a very pretty dilemma: I must commit murder or commit matrimony! Which is best, now? a licence from Doctors' Commons, or a sentence from the Old Bailey? If I kill my màn, the law hangs me; if I marry my woman, I shall hang myself. – But, damn it! cowards dare fight; I'll marry! That's the most daring action of the two. So, my dear cousin Angelica, have at you.

> *Exit.*

Scene Two

Newgate. Clincher Senior solus.

CLINCHER SENIOR.

How severe and melancholy are Newgate reflections! Last week my father died; yesterday I turned beau; today I am laid by the heels, and tomorrow shall be hung by the neck. – I was agreeing with a bookseller about printing an account of my journey through France to Italy; but now, the history of my travels through Holborn to Tyburn – 'The last and dying speech of Beau Clincher, that was going to the Jubilee. – Come, a halfpenny apiece!' – A sad sound, a sad sound, faith!

'Tis one way to have a man's death make a great noise in the world.

Enter Smuggler and Jailer.

SMUGGLER.

Well, friend, I have told you who I am: so send these letters into Thames Street, as directed; they are to gentlemen that will bail me. –

Exit Jailer.

Eh! this Newgate is a very populous place: here's robbery and repentance in every corner. – Well, friend, what are you? a cut-throat or a burn-bailiff?

CLINCHER SENIOR.

What are you, mistress? a bawd or a witch? Hark'ee, if you are a witch, d'ye see, I'll give you a hundred pounds to mount me on a broom-staff and whip me away to the Jubilee.

SMUGGLER.

The Jubilee! Oh, you young rakehell, what brought you here?

CLINCHER SENIOR.

Ah, you old rogue, what brought you here, if you go to that.

SMUGGLER.

I knew, sir, what your powdering, your prinking, your dancing, and your frisking, would come to.

CLINCHER SENIOR.

And I knew what your cozening, your extortion, and your smuggling would come to.

SMUGGLER.

Ay, sir, and you must break your indentures, and run to the devil in petticoats? You design to swing in masquerade, master, d'ye?

CLINCHER SENIOR.

Ay, sir, and you must go to the plays, too, sirrah! Lord! Lord what business has a 'prentice at a playhouse, unless it be to hear his master made a cuckold, and his mistress a whore! 'Tis ten to one now, but some malicious poet has my character upon the stage within this month. 'Tis a hard matter now that an honest sober man can't sin in private for this plaguy stage. I gave an honest gentleman five guineas myself towards writing a book against it: and it has done no good, we see.

CLINCHER SENIOR.

Well, well, master, take courage; our comfort is, we have lived together: only with this difference, that I have lived like a fool, and shall die like a knave; and you have lived like a knave and shall die like a fool.

SMUGGLER.

No, sirrah! I have sent a messenger for my clothes, and shall get out immediately, and shall be upon your jury by-and-by. – Go to prayers, you rogue! go to prayers!

Exit.

CLINCHER SENIOR.

Prayers! 'tis a hard taking when a man must say grace to the gallows. Ah, this cursed intriguing! Had I swung handsomely in a silken garter now, I had died in my duty; but to hang in hemp, like the vulgar, 'tis very ungenteel.

Enter Tom Errand.

A reprieve! a reprieve! Thou dear, dear – damned rogue, where have you been? Thou art the most welcome – son of a whore! Where's my clothes?

ERRAND.

Sir, I see where mine are: come, sir, strip, sir, strip!

CLINCHER SENIOR.

What, sir! will you abuse a gentleman?

ERRAND.

A gentleman! ha, ha, ha! D'ye know where you are, sir? We're all gentlemen here. I stand up for liberty and property. Newgate's a commonwealth. No courtier has business among us. Come, sir!

CLINCHER SENIOR.

Well, but stay, stay till I send for my own clothes: I shall get out presently.

ERRAND.

No, no, sir! I'll ha' you into the dungeon, and uncase you.

CLINCHER SENIOR.

Sir, you can't master me; for I'm twenty thousand strong.

Exeunt struggling.

Scene Three

Lady Darling's house. Enter Wildair with letters, footmen following.

SIR HARRY.

Here, fly all around, and bear these as directed; – you to Westminster, you to St. James's, and you into the City. Tell all my friends a bridegroom's joy invites their presence. Look all of ye like bridegrooms also: all appear with hospitable looks, and bear a welcome in your faces. Tell 'em I'm married. If any ask to whom, make no reply, but tell 'em that I'm married, that joy shall crown the day, and love the night. Begone! fly!

Exeunt Footmen.

Enter Standard.

A thousand welcomes, friend! My pleasure's now complete, since I can share it with my friend. Brisk joy shall bound from me to you; then back again; and like the sun grow warmer by reflection!

STANDARD.
You're always pleasant, Sir Harry; but this transcends yourself! Whence proceeds it?

SIR HARRY.
Canst thou not guess, my friend? Whence flows all earthly joy? What is the life of man and soul of pleasure? – woman! What fires the heart with transport, and the soul with raptures? – lovely woman! What is the master-stroke and smile of the creation, but charming, virtuous woman? When nature, in the general composition, first brought woman forth, like a flushed poet ravished with his fancy, with ecstasy she blessed the fair production! – Methinks, my friend, you relish not my joy; what is the cause?

STANDARD.
Canst thou not guess? What is the bane of man and scourge of life, but woman? What is the heathenish idol man sets up, and is damned for worshipping? – treacherous woman. What are those, whose eyes, like basilisks, shine beautiful for sure destruction, whose smiles are dangerous as the grin of fiends, but false, deluding woman? Woman! whose composition inverts humanity: their body's heavenly, but their souls are clay!

SIR HARRY.
Come, come, Colonel, this is too much. I know your wrongs received from Lurewell may excuse your resentments against her: but 'tis unpardonable to charge the failings of a single woman upon the whole sex. I have found one, whose virtues –

STANDARD.
So have I, Sir Harry; I have found one, whose pride's above yielding to a prince. And if lying, dissembling, perjury, and falsehood, be no breaches in woman's honour, she's as innocent as infancy.

SIR HARRY.
Well, Colonel, I find your opinion grows stronger by opposition: I shall now therefore waive the argument, and only beg you for this day to make a show of complaisance at least. – Here comes my charming bride.

Enter Lady Darling and Angelica.

STANDARD (*saluting Angelica*).
I wish you, madam, all the joys of love and fortune.

Enter Clincher Junior.

CLINCHER JUNIOR.
Gentlemen and ladies, I'm just upon the spur, and have only a minute to take my leave.

SIR HARRY.
Whither are you bound, sir?

CLINCHER JUNIOR.
Bound, sir! I'm going to the Jubilee, sir.

LADY DARLING.
Bless me, cousin! how came you by these clothes?

CLINCHER JUNIOR.
Clothes! ha, ha, ha! the rarest jest! ha, ha, ha! I shall burst, by Jupiter Ammon, I shall burst!

LADY DARLING.
What's the matter, cousin?

CLINCHER JUNIOR.
The matter! ha, ha, ha! Why, an honest porter – ha, ha, ha! – has knocked out my brother's brains, ha, ha, ha!

SIR HARRY.
A very good jest, i' faith! ha, ha, ha!

CLINCHER JUNIOR.
Ay, sir, but the best jest of all is, he knocked out my brother's brains with a hammer, and so he is as dead as a door-nail, ha, ha, ha!

LADY DARLING.
And do you laugh, wretch?

CLINCHER JUNIOR.
Laugh! ha, ha, ha! – Let me see e'er a younger brother in England that won't laugh at such a jest.

ANGELICA.
You appeared a very sober pious gentleman some hours ago.

CLINCHER JUNIOR.
Psha! I was a fool then; but now, madam, I'm a wit: I can rake now. As for your part, madam, you might have had me once: but now, madam, if you should chance fall to eating chalk, or gnawing the sheets, 'tis none of my fault. Now, madam, I have got an estate, and I must go to the Jubilee.

Enter Clincher Senior in a blanket.

CLINCHER SENIOR.
Must you so, rogue? must ye? – You will go to the Jubilee, will you?

CLINCHER JUNIOR.
A ghost! a ghost! – Send for the dean and chapter presently.

CLINCHER SENIOR.
A ghost! no, no, sirrah; I'm an elder brother, rogue!

CLINCHER JUNIOR.
I don't care a farthing for that; I'm sure you're dead in law.
CLINCHER SENIOR.
Why so, sirrah? why so?

CLINCHER JUNIOR.
Because, sir, I can get a fellow to swear he knocked out your brains.

SIR HARRY.
An odd way of swearing a man out of his life!

CLINCHER JUNIOR.
Smell him, gentlemen; he has a deadly scent about him!

CLINCHER SENIOR.
Truly, the apprehensions of death may have made me savour a little! (*Aside.*) O Lord! the colonel! – The apprehension of him may make me savour worse, I'm afraid.

CLINCHER JUNIOR.
In short, sir, were you ghost, or brother, or devil, I will go to the Jubilee, by Jupiter Ammon!

STANDARD.
Go to the Jubilee! go to the bear-garden! The travel of such fools as you doubly injures our country; you expose our native follies, which ridicules us among strangers; and return fraught only with their vices, which you vend here for fashionable gallantry. A travelling fool is as dangerous as a home-bred villain. Get ye to your native plough and cart; converse with animals like yourselves – sheep and oxen; men are creatures that you don't understand.

SIR HARRY.
Let 'em alone, Colonel, their folly will be now diverting. – Come, gentlemen, we'll dispute this point some other time; I hear some fiddles tuning, let's hear how they can entertain us. – Be pleased to sit.

Here singing and dancing; after which a Footman enters and whispers Wildair.

SIR HARRY (*to Lady Darling*).
Madam, shall I beg you to entertain the company in the next room for a moment?

LADY DARLING.
With all my heart – Come, gentlemen.

Exeunt Omnes but Wildair.

SIR HARRY.
A lady to inquire for me! Who can this be?

Enter Lady Lurewell.

Oh, madam, this favour is beyond my expectation, to come uninvited to dance at my wedding! – What d'ye gaze at, madam?

LADY LUREWELL.
A monster! – If thou art married, thou'rt the most perjured wretch that e'er avouched deceit!

SIR HARRY.
Heyday! why, madam, I'm sure I never swore to marry you! I made, indeed, a slight promise, upon condition of your granting me a small favour; but you would not consent, you know.

LADY LUREWELL (*aside*).
How he upbraids me with my shame! – (*Aloud.*) Can you deny your binding vows. When this appears a witness 'gainst your falsehood?

Showing a ring.

Methinks the motto of this sacred pledge
Should flash confusion in your guilty face!
Read!
Read here the binding words of *Love and Honour*;
Words not unknown to your perfidious eyes,
Though utter strangers to your treacherous heart!

SIR HARRY.
The woman's stark staring mad, that's certain!

LADY LUREWELL.

Was it maliciously designed to let me find my misery when past redress? to let me know you, only to know you false? Had not cursed chance showed me the surprising motto, I had been happy. The first knowledge I had of you was fatal to me, and this second worse.

SIR HARRY.

What the devil's all this! Madam, I'm not at leisure for raillery at present; I have weighty affairs upon my hands; the business of pleasure, madam – Any other time –

Going.

LADY LUREWELL.

Stay, I conjure you, stay!

SIR HARRY.

Faith, I can't! my bride expects me. – But hark'ee when the honeymoon is over, about a month or two hence, I may do you a small favour.

Exit.

LADY LUREWELL.

Grant me some wild expressions, Heavens, or I shall burst! Woman's weakness, man's falsehood, my own shame, and love's disdain, at once swell up my breast! – Words, words, or I shall burst!

Going.

Re-enter Standard.

STANDARD.

Stay, madam, you need not shun my sight; for if you are perfect woman, you have confidence to outface a crime, and bear the charge of guilt without a blush.

LADY LUREWELL.

The charge of guilt! – What, making a fool of you? I've done't, and glory in the act! the height of female justice were to make you all hang or drown! Dissembling to the prejudice of men is virtue; and every look, or sign, or smile, or tear that can deceive is meritorious.

STANDARD.

Very pretty principles truly! If there be truth in woman, 'tis now in thee. – Come, madam, you know that you're dis-covered, and being sensible you can't escape, you would now turn to bay. – That ring, madam, proclaims you guilty.

LADY LUREWELL.

O monster! villain! perfidious villain! has he told you?

STANDARD.

I'll tell it you, and loudly too.

LADY LUREWELL.

Oh, name it not! – Yes, speak it out, 'tis so just a punishment for putting faith in man, that I will bear it all; and let credulous maids, that trust their honour to the tongues of men, thus hear their shame proclaimed. – Speak now what his busy scandal, and your improving malice, both dare utter.

STANDARD.

Your falsehood can't be reached by malice nor by satire; your actions are the justest libel on your fame. Your words, your looks, your tears, I did believe in spite of common fame: nay, 'gainst my own eyes I still maintained your truth. I imagined Wildair's boasting of your favours to be the pure result of his own vanity. At last he urged your taking presents of him; as a convincing proof of which you yesterday from him received that ring: – which ring, that I might be sure he gave it, I lent him for that purpose.

LADY LUREWELL.

Ha! you lent him for that purpose?

STANDARD.

Yes, yes, madam, I lent him for that purpose – no denying it. – I know it well, for I have worn it long, and desire you now, madam, to restore it to the just owner.

LADY LUREWELL.

The just owner! Think, sir, think but of what importance 'tis to own it. If you have love and honour in your soul, 'tis then most justly yours; if not, you are a robber, and have stolen it basely.

STANDARD.

Ha! your words, like meeting flints, have struck a light to show me something strange. – But tell me instantly, is not your real name Manly?

LADY LUREWELL.

Answer me first: did not you receive this ring about twelve years ago?

STANDARD.

I did.

LADY LUREWELL.

And were not you about that time entertained two nights at the house of Sir Oliver Manly in Oxfordshire?

STANDARD.

I was ! I was! – (*Runs to her, and embraces her.*) The blest

remembrance fires my soul with transport! I know the rest –
you are the charming she, and I the happy man.

LADY LUREWELL.

How has blind Fortune stumbled on the right! – 'Twas cruel
to forsake me.

STANDARD.

The particulars of my fortune were too tedious now; but to
discharge myself from the stain of dishonour, I must tell you,
that immediately upon my return to the university, my elder
brother and I quarrelled. My father, to prevent farther mischief, posts me away to travel: I writ to you from London, but
fear the letter came not to your hands.

LADY LUREWELL.

I never had the least account of you, by letter or otherwise.

STANDARD.

Three years I lived abroad, and at my return, found you were
gone out of the kingdom; though none could tell me whither.
Missing you thus, I went to Flanders, served my king till the
peace commenced; then fortunately going on board at
Amsterdam, one ship transported us both to England. At the
first sight I loved, though ignorant of the hidden cause. – You
may remember, madam, that talking once of marriage, I told
you I was engaged; to your dear self I meant.

LADY LUREWELL.

Then men are still most generous and brave – and to reward
your truth, an estate of three thousand pounds a year waits
your acceptance; and if I can satisfy you in my past conduct,
and the reasons that engaged me to deceive all men, I shall
expect the honourable performance of your promise, and that
you would stay with me in England.

STANDARD.

Stay! – not fame nor glory e'er shall part us more. My honour
can be nowhere more concerned than here.

Re-enter Wildair, Angelica, both Clinchers.

O Sir Harry, Fortune has acted miracles! The story's strange
and tedious, but all amounts to this: that woman's mind is
charming as her person, and I am made a convert too to
beauty.

SIR HARRY.

I wanted only this to make my pleasure perfect.

Enter Smuggler.

SMUGGLER.

So, gentlemen and ladies, is my gracious nephew Vizard
among ye?

SIR HARRY.

Sir, he dares not show his face among such honourable
company, for your gracious nephew is –

SMUGGLER.

What, sir? Have a care what you say –

SIR HARRY.

A villain, sir.

SMUGGLER.

With all my heart: – I'll pardon you the beating me for that
very word. And pray, Sir Harry, when you see him next, tell
him this news from me, that I have disinherited him, that I
will leave him as poor as a disbanded quartermaster. And this
is the positive and stiff resolution of threescore and ten; an age
that sticks as obstinately to its purpose, as to the old fashion of
its cloak.

SIR HARRY (*to Angelica*).

You see, madam, how industriously Fortune has punished his
offence to you.

ANGELICA.

I can scarcely, sir, reckon it an offence, considering the happy
consequence of it.

SMUGGLER.

O Sir Harry, he is as hypocritical –

LADY LUREWELL.

As yourself, Mr Alderman: how fares my good old nurse,
pray, sir?

SMUGGLER.

O madam, I shall be even with you before I part with your
writings and money, that I have in my hands!

STANDARD.

A word with you, Mr Alderman: do you kow this pocket-
book?

SMUGGLER (*aside*).

O Lord, it contains an account of all my secret practices in
trading! – (*Aloud.*) How came you by it, sir?

STANDARD.

Sir Harry here dusted it out of your pocket, at this lady's
house yesterday. It contains an account of some secret
practices in your merchandizing; among the rest, the counter-

part of an agreement with a correspondent at Bordeaux, about transporting French wine in Spanish casks. – First return this lady all her writings, then I shall consider whether I shall lay your proceedings before the parliament or not; whose justice will never suffer your smuggling to go unpunished.

SMUGGLER.

Oh, my poor ship and cargo!

CLINCHER SENIOR.

Hark'ee, master, you had as good come along with me to the Jubilee now.

ANGELICA.

Come, Mr Alderman, for once let a woman advise. Would you be thought an honest man, banish covetousness, that worst gout of age; avarice is a poor pilfering quality of the soul, and will as certainly cheat, as a thief would steal. – Would you be thought a reformer of the times, be less severe in your censures, less rigid in your precepts, and more strict in your example.

SIR HARRY.

Right, madam; virtue flows freer from imitation than compulsion; of which, Colonel, your conversion and mine are just examples.
In vain are musty morals taught in schools,
By rigid teachers, and as rigid rules,
Where virtue with a frowning aspect stands,
And frights the pupil from its rough commands.
But woman, –
Charming woman, can true converts make;
We love the precepts for the teacher's sake.
Virtue in them appears so bright, so gay,
We hear with transport, and with pride obey.

EPILOGUE

SIR HARRY.
Now all depart, each his respective way,
To spend an evening's chat upon the play;
Some to Hippolito's; one homeward goes,
And one with loving she retires to th' Rose.
The amorous pair, in all things frank and free,
Perhaps my say the play – in Number Three.
The tearing spark, if Phillis aught gainsays,
Breaks th' drawer's head, kicks her, and murders Bays.
To coffee some retreat to save their pockets,
Others, more generous, damn the play at Locket's;
But there, I hope, the author's fears are vain,
Malice ne'er spoke in generous champagne.
That poet merits an ignoble death,
Who fears to fall over a brave Monteth.
The privilege of wine we only ask,
You'll taste again before you damn the flask.
Our author fears not you; but those he may,
Who in cold blood murder a man in tea:
Those men of spleen who, fond the world should know it,
Sit down and for their twopence damn a poet.
Their criticism's good, that we can say for't.
From box to stage, from stage to box they run,
First steal the play, then damn it when they've done.
But now, to know what fate may us betide,
Among our friends, in Cornhill and Cheapside:
But those, I think, have but one rule for plays;
They'll say they're good, if so the world says.
If it should please them, and their spouses know it,
They straight inquire what kind of man's the poet.
But from side-box we dread a fearful doom,
All the good-natured beaux are gone to Rome.
The ladies' censure I'd almost forgot,
Then for a line or two t' engage their vote:
But that way's old, below our author's aim,
No less than his whole play is a compliment to them.
For their sakes then the play can't miss succeeding,
Though critics may want wit, they have good breeding.
They won't I'm sure, forfeit the ladies' graces,
By showing their ill-nature to their faces,
Our business with good manners may be done,
Flatter us here, and damn us when you're gone.